# New Testament Greek to Hebrew Dictionary

~~~~~~~~~~~~~~~~~~~~~~~~~~~~~~~~~~~~~~~~~~

### 500 Greek Words and Names
### Retranslated Back into Hebrew for
### English Readers

By Jeff A. Benner

Cover design by Jeff A. Benner.

"New Testament Greek to Hebrew Dictionary," by Jeff A. Benner.
ISBN 978-1-60264-749-7.

Published 2011 by Virtualbookworm.com Publishing Inc., P.O. Box
9949, College Station, TX 77845, US. ©2011, Jeff A. Benner. All rights
reserved. Any part of this book may be copied for educational
purposes only, without prior permission.

Manufactured in the United States of America.

# Table of Contents

# Acknowledgments

I would like to thank a group of people who have sacrificed of their time and talents to make corrections and suggestions for this book. Without them, this book would not be the quality that it is. My heartfelt thanks go out to each of these individuals.

| | |
|---|---|
| Holly Begley | Jeanne Irons |
| LuAna Craig | Jerry Lambert |
| Bea Baldridge | Paul Lurk |
| Rob Black | Matthew R. Mencel |
| Jordan Day | Frances Stolz |
| Bob Fier | Randy Talbot |
| Jason Harris | Dennis Wenrick |
| Gordon Hayes | Janet Wyckoff |
| Myhrrhleine Hunter | Liz Zeller |

# Introduction

## Hebrew in the First Century

The purpose of this book is to be a guide for translating the Greek words of the New Testament into Hebrew. Why translate the Greek New Testament into Hebrew? While the oldest manuscripts of the New Testament are in Greek, it is unlikely Yeshua[1] or his Talmidim[2] taught in Greek, but instead in Hebrew. Even if these teachings were first "written" in Greek, they are still a translation of the Hebrew that they "spoke." Because the New Testament was first written by Jews who spoke and wrote Hebrew, for Jews who also spoke and read Hebrew, it stands to reason that they would have written in Hebrew. Archaeological evidence to support this view can be found in the Dead Sea Scrolls, texts contemporary to the New Testament period, which included writings similar to the New Testament that were written in Hebrew.

Found within the book of Acts is the most compelling evidence that the writers of the New Testament spoke Hebrew.

---

[1] The Hebrew name that is transliterated into Greek as ιησους and into English as Jesus.

[2] A Hebrew word meaning "students," where the Greek counterpart, μαθητης, is usually translated as "disciples."

3

*And as Paul was about to be brought into the castle, he saith unto the chief captain, May I say something unto thee? And he said, Dost thou know Greek? (Acts 21:37, ASV)*

In this passage Paul is speaking to the captain in Greek, but the captain is surprised that he knows Greek. Why would the captain be so surprised that Paul spoke Greek if everyone spoke Greek? Evidently, Greek was not the language of all people at this time. After speaking with the captain, Paul turns to the crowd and then speaks to them in "Hebrew."

*And when he had given him leave, Paul, standing on the stairs, beckoned with the hand unto the people; and when there was made a great silence, he spake unto them in the Hebrew language, saying, (Acts 21:40, ASV)*

Josephus, the Jewish historian, gives us a glimpse of the Jewish attitude toward the Greek language.

*"I have also taken a great deal of pains to obtain the learning of the Greeks, and understanding the elements of the Greek language although I have so long accustomed myself to speak our own language, that I cannot pronounce Greek with sufficient exactness: for our nation does not encourage those that learn the languages of many nations". (Josephus, Ant.20.11.2)*

The *Oxford Dictionary of the Christian Church* stated in its first edition in 1958, "Hebrew ceased to be a spoken language around the fourth century BC"[3]. However, upon new linguistic and archaeological evidence, the *Oxford Dictionary of the Christian Church* now says in its third edition in 1997, "Hebrew continued to be used as a spoken and written language in the New Testament period"[4].

The most significant evidence for a Hebrew New Testament is found within the text itself where we find many Hebraisms[5]. A very common Hebraism is the use of similar sounding words together such as we find in the following verse.

> ...*God is able of these stones (Hebrew-ebeniym) to raise up children (Hebrew-beniym) unto Abraham. (Matthew 3:9, KJV)*

These "word puns" are not isolated incidents, but are found throughout the text when it is retranslated back into Hebrew.

Since the Greek text of the New Testament is merely a translation of the Hebrew, in order to accurately read and understand the text we must retranslate the Greek back into Hebrew. And then take our definitions of these words from the Hebrew.

---

[3] "Hebrew" in The Oxford Dictionary of the Christian Church, editor F.L. Cross, first edition (Oxford, 1958)
[4] "Hebrew" in The Oxford Dictionary of the Christian Church, editor F.L. Cross, third edition (Oxford 1997).
[5] Text that is characteristic of the Hebrew language.

## About Strong's Numbers

The "Strong's" numbering system, which is used in this book, was developed by James Strong in the late nineteenth century. This numbering system assigns a unique number to each Hebrew word found in the Old Testament and each Greek word found in the New Testament. James Strong, in his book *Strong's Exhaustive Concordance of the Bible*, connected each word in the King James Version of the Bible with the number of the Hebrew or Greek word that English word is translating. For instance, in John 1:1 the word "beginning" is a translation of the Greek word αρχη (ar-khay), which James Strong had assigned the number 746. When you look up the Strong's Greek number 746 in this book you find that the equivalent Hebrew word is Strong's Hebrew number 7225, which is ראשית (rey-shit), meaning "summit." The following is the *Strong's Exhaustive Concordance* entries for the word "beginning" (in the far right column are the Strong's numbers).

**Beginning**

| | | | | |
|---|---|---|---|---|
| Mat | 14 | 30 | and b. to sink | 756 |
| Mat | 19 | 4 | at the b. made them | 746 |
| Mat | 19 | 8 | but from the b. it was | 746 |
| Mat | 20 | 8 | from the last unto | 756 |
| | | | *...some entries removed for brevity...* | |
| Joh | 1 | 1 | In the b. was the Word | 746 |
| Joh | 1 | 2 | was in the b. with God | 746 |
| Joh | 2 | 10 | man at the b. doth set | 4412 |
| Joh | 2 | 11 | This b. of miracles did | 746 |
| | | | *...additional entries removed for brevity...* | |

# New Testament Greek to Hebrew Dictionary

As you can see, there are three different Strong's numbers (746, 756 and 4412) associated with the English word "beginning." This means that there are three different Greek words translated as "beginning" in the King James Version of the Bible. Strong's Greek number 746 is the Greek word αρχη (ar-khay), which we have already seen is equivalent to the Hebrew word ראשית (rey-shit) meaning "summit." Strong's Greek number 756 is the Greek word αρχομαι (ar-khom-ahee), which is equivalent to the Hebrew word חלל (hha-lal) meaning "pierce." Strong's Greek number 4412 is the Greek word πρωτον (pro-ton), which is equivalent to the Hebrew word ריאשון (ri-shon) meaning "first."

Besides *Strong's Exhaustive Concordance*, there are a number of Bible software programs[6] and on-line programs[7] that will allow you to find the Strong's number of any given word in your English Bible.

## Methods of translating NT Greek back into Hebrew

The first and most helpful method of translating Greek into Hebrew is by using the Septuagint[8] as a dictionary. As an

---

[6] Such as the free E-Sword program (http://www.e-sword.net).
[7] Such as the Blue Letter Bible (http://www.blueletterbible.org).
[8] The Septuagint is a Greek translation of the Old Testament written by Jews between the third and first centuries BC.

example, in the Septuagint of Genesis 2:3 we find the phrase και ηυλογησεν ο θεος (*kai eulogesen ho theos*), which is a translation of the Hebrew phrase ויברך אלהים (*vai'yevarekh elohiym*). From this, we learn that the Greek verb ευλογεω (*eulogeo*) is a translation of the Hebrew verb ברך (*barakh*) and the Greek noun θεος (*theos*) is a translation of the Hebrew noun אלהים (*elohiym*).

The second method is as simple as determining the meaning of a given Greek word and selecting the Hebrew word with the same meaning. For instance, the Greek noun αγγελος (*angelos*) means "messenger," which is the exact same definition of the Hebrew noun מלאך (*malakh*).

**The selection of Greek words in the Dictionary**

This dictionary includes the five hundred most common words and names found in the Greek New Testament: 449 words (200 verbs, 190 nouns, 50 adjectives and nine adverbs) and 51 names.

Only the most common Hebrew words that are associated with a given Greek word have been selected for this dictionary. For example, in the Septuagint, the Greek verb διωκω (*dioko*) is used 53 times. It is used 38 times as a translation of the Hebrew verb רדף (*radaph*, Strong's Heb. #7291) and 4 times for רוץ (*ruts*, Strong's Heb. #7323). In

8

addition, this same Greek verb is used 11 other times to translate 9 other Hebrew verbs[9]. In order to keep this dictionary simple, this dictionary will only list רדף and רוץ with the Greek verb διωκω.

A few Greek words, whose frequency count would have allowed for them to be added to this dictionary, were not added, as there are no Biblical Hebrew words with the same meaning. For instance, the Greek word παρρεσια (*parrasisa*, Strong's Grk. #3954) has the meaning "boldness of speech." However, there is no Biblical Hebrew word with this meaning, nor is this Greek word found in the Septuagint[10] and therefore this Greek word will not be found in this dictionary.

This dictionary does not include pronouns, particles, prepositions, articles, conjunctions or copulas[11].

There are a few Greek words in the New Testament that are not found, or are rarely found, in the Greek of the Septuagint. A good example of this is the Greek word σταυροω (stauroo, Strong's Grk. #4717), which in the New Testament is

---

[9] שדד and נוס, נדף, חרד, חרד, חרבה, הלך, רמה, דיר.

[10] Some might question how a Greek word could be found in the New Testament if it is a translation of the Hebrew. In the Septuagint we find many instances where the translator embellished on the text by inserting Greek words, more as an interpretation than an actual translation.

[11] Verbs that are equivalent to the English verb "to be."

translated as "crucify," but is only found once in the Septuagint, Esther 7:9, where it is used for the translation of the Hebrew word תלה (talah, Strong's Heb. #8518), usually translated into English as "hang." In cases such as this I consulted other Semitic New Testaments[12] for the Hebrew or Aramaic words that were used for these difficult Greek words.

## The differences between Greek and Hebrew

One of the major differences between Greek and Hebrew is its philosophy. Greek is a very abstract language, while Hebrew is much more concrete. An example is the Greek word πιστις (*pistis*, Strong's Grk. #4102), which means "faith," an intellectual acceptance of what is true, a very abstract term. This Greek word is the translation of the Hebrew אמונה (*emunah*, Strong's Heb. #530), which literally means firm, securely fixed in place[13].

Both Greek and Hebrew use words to express literal and figurative concepts, but Hebrew much more so.

*Even so every good tree bringeth forth good fruit; but the corrupt tree bringeth forth evil fruit. A good tree*

---

[12] Such as the Shem Tov Hebrew of Matthew, the Aramaic Peshitta and the Salkinson-Ginsburg Hebrew translation of the Greek New Testament.
[13] The concrete nature of this Hebrew word can be seen in Exodus 17:12 where it is translated as "steady."

*cannot bring forth evil fruit, neither can a corrupt tree bring forth good fruit. Every tree that bringeth not forth good fruit is hewn down, and cast into the fire. Therefore by their fruits ye shall know them. (Matthew 7:17-20, ASV)*

In this passage Yeshua uses the word fruit in a literal sense, but also in a figurative sense as the fruit of false prophets. In some cases, such as the one just demonstrated, we are familiar with the figurative use of a word, but in other cases we are not. Genesis 13:2 says that Abram was very "heavy." In our modern western way of thinking a "heavy" man is an obese one, but the Hebrew word כבד (*kaveyd*, Strong's Heb. #3515) can mean heavy in possessions (rich) or heavy in authority (honor).

While a Hebrew word may have multiple meanings, the Greek word used to translate that Hebrew word may be more limited in its meaning. This means that the translator chose one Greek word over another for the original Hebrew word, but opens the possibility for a different interpretation. A good example of this can be found in the book of Matthew.

*Blessed are the poor in spirit... (Matthew 5:3)*

The Greek word for "poor" is πτωχος (*ptoksos*, Strong's Grk. #4434) meaning "poor" in the sense of being "beggarly." Three Hebrew words have the same meaning, but one of them, עני (*ani*, Strong's Heb. #6041), can also mean afflicted.

This interpretation fits more contextually with the passage than "beggardly."

Another difference between Greek and Hebrew is the definition of verbs, nouns and adjectives. In Hebrew, both verbs and nouns are action oriented. The verb describes the action of someone or something while the noun describes someone or something performing an action. For instance, the Hebrew word מלך (*melekh*) can be a verb (Strong's Heb. #4427) meaning "to rule" or a noun (Strong's Heb. #4428) meaning "the one who rules (a king)." Hebrew also sometimes uses the same words for nouns and adjectives. For instance, the Hebrew word צדיק (*tsadiq*, Strong's Heb. #6662) can mean steadfast (an adjective) or one who is steadfast (a noun).

## How to use the New Testament Greek to Hebrew Dictionary

While this book will not enable you to do a complete retranslation of whole passages, it will provide a retranslating of specific words. Because the Greek and Hebrew languages are so vastly different, we will often find, after retranslating Greek words back into Hebrew, a very different interpretation of a passage.

Let's begin by examining some of the words in the following passage.

*Master, which is the great commandment in the law?*
*(Matthew 22:36, KJV)*

When we look up the word "master" in a Strong's concordance we find that it is the Greek word διδασκαλος (*didaskalos*, Strong's Grk. #1320). When we look up this Greek word in this dictionary, we find that this Greek word is a translation of the Hebrew words למד (*lamed*, Strong's Heb. #3925) and מורה (*moreh*, Strong's Heb. #4175), both meaning "teacher."

When we follow the same process for the word "commandment," we find it is the Greek word εντολη (*entole*, Strong's Grk. #1785), whose equivelant in Hebrew is מצוה (*mitsvah*, Strong's Heb. #4687) meaning "directive." The word "law" is the Greek word νομος (*nomos*, Strong's Grk. #3551), whose equivelant in Hebrew is תורה (*torah*, Strong's Heb. #8451) meaning "teaching." When we retranslate this verse back into Hebrew we have, "Teacher, what is the great directive in the teaching"?

As we can see, the KJV translation of the Greek implies that the speaker is looking for one command out of all the others that is the greatest (best). By examining the Hebrew behind the Greek we find that this is not the case. The speaker is looking for the directive (the goal) that can be found within the teachings.

Here are the results of a couple of other verses.

*And saying, The time is fulfilled, and the kingdom of God is at hand: repent ye, and believe the gospel. (Mark 1:15, KJV)*

| KJV | Grk # | Heb # | Translation |
| --- | --- | --- | --- |
| Time | 2540 | 4150 | Appointed time |
| Fulfilled | 4137 | 4930 | Fulfill |
| Kingdom | 932 | 4438 | Empire |
| God | 2316 | 430 | Elohiym |
| Hand | 1448 | 5066 | Draw near |
| Repent | 3340 | 5162 | Be comforted |
| Believe | 4100 | 539 | Support |
| Gospel | 2098 | 1309 | Good news |

When this verse is retranslated back into Hebrew it reads: *"And saying, the appointed time is fulfilled, and the empire of Elohiym is brought near: be comforted and support the report of the good news."*

*For Christ is the end of the law for righteousness to every one that believeth. (Romans 10:4, KJV)*

| KJV | Grk # | Heb # | Translation |
| --- | --- | --- | --- |
| Christ | 5547 | 4899 | Annointed one |
| End | 5056 | 7097 | Extremity |

14

| Law | 3551 | 8451 | Teaching |
| Righteousness | 1343 | 6664 | Steadfast |
| Believeth | 4100 | 539 | Support |

When this verse is retranslated back into Hebrew it reads; *"For the anointed one is the extremity of the teaching for being steadfast on the path to all that support it."*

Once the Hebrew Strong's number is found for any given Greek word, further study can be done by using the concordance to look up this Hebrew word in the Old Testament to examine the context of how it is used. It also would be a good idea to look this word up in other Hebrew dictionaries[14] to search out its fuller meaning.

To get you started with using this book, the Book of James has been added after the dictionary, which includes the Greek Strong's numbers for each word within the book.

---

[14] Such as; Vine's Dictionary, Thayer's Dictionary, Gesenius' Lexicon, BDB Lexicon or the Ancient Hebrew Lexicon of the Bible.

# New Testament Greek to Hebrew Dictionary

# Dictionary

**Grk#:**11 Αβρααμ / ab-rah-am *(name)*: Abraham *Freq:* 73
   **Heb#:**85 אברהם / av-ra-ham *(name)*: Avraham—A personal name of Hebrew origin meaning "Father lifted up."

**Grk#:**18 αγαθος / ag-ath-os *(adj)*: Good *Freq:* 102
   **Heb#:**2896 טוב / tov *(noun)*: Functional—Fulfilling the action for which a person or thing is specially fitted or used, or for which a thing exists. A functioning within its intended purpose.

**Grk#:**25 αγαπαω / ag-ap-ah-o *(verb)*: Love *Freq:* 142
   **Heb#:**157 אהב / a-hav *(verb)*: Love—To provide and protect that which is given as a privilege. An intimacy of action and emotion. Strong affection for another arising from personal ties.

**Grk#:**26 αγαπη / ag-ah-pay *(noun)*: Love *Freq:* 116
   **Heb#:**160 אהבה / a-ha-vah *(noun)*: Affection—A moderate feeling or emotion. A tender attachment or fondness.

**Grk#:**27 αγαπητος / ag-ap-ay-tos *(adj)*: Beloved *Freq:* 22
   **Heb#:**3039 ידיד / ya-did *(noun)*: Beloved—One who is loved.

17

**Grk#:32** αγγελος / ang-el-os *(noun)*: Messenger *Freq: 186*
    **Heb#:4397** מלאך / mal-akh *(noun)*: Messenger—One who bears a message or runs an errand. One who walks for another.

**Grk#:37** αγιαζω / hag-ee-ad-zo *(verb)*: Sanctify *Freq: 29*
    **Heb#:6942** קדש / qa-dash *(verb)*: Set apart—To move or place someone or something separate from the whole for a special purpose.

**Grk#:50** αγνοεω / ag-no-eh-o *(verb)*: Be Ignorant *Freq: 31*
    **Heb#:3045** ידע / ya-da *(verb)*: Know—To have an intimate and personal understanding; to have an intimate relationship with another person, usually sexual. {The Greek word αγνοεω is a translation of the Hebrew verb ידע when it is preceded by the word לא (*lo,* Strong's Heb. #3808) meaning "not knowing."}

**Grk#:59** αγοραζω / ag-or-ad-zo *(verb)*: Buy *Freq: 31*
    **Heb#:7666** שבל / sha-val *(verb)*: Exchange—The act of giving or taking one thing in return for another. To buy or sell produce, usually grain. To barter.

**Grk#:68** αγρος / ag-ros *(noun)*: Field *Freq: 36*
    **Heb#:7704** שדה / sa-deh *(noun)*: Field—An open land area free of trees and buildings. A level plot of ground.

**Grk#:71** αγω / ag-o *(verb)*: Bring *Freq: 72*
    **Heb#:935** בוא / bo *(verb)*: Come—To move toward something; approach; enter. This can be understood as to come or to go. {The Greek word αγω is a translation of

the hiphil (causative) form of the Hebrew verb בוא
meaning "to make come," or "bring."}

**Grk#:**79 αδελφη / ad-el-fay *(noun)*: Sister *Freq:* 24
  **Heb#:**269 אחות / a-hhot *(noun)*: Sister— A female who
  shares at least one parent with another.

**Grk#:**80 αδελφος / ad-el-fos *(noun)*: Brother *Freq:* 346
  **Heb#:**251 אח / ahh *(noun)*: Brother— A male who shares
  at least one parent with another. One who stands
  between the enemy and the family; a protector.

**Grk#:**91 αδικεω / ad-ee-keh-o *(verb)*: Hurt *Freq:* 28
  **Heb#:**2555 חמס / hha-mas *(noun)*: Violence—Exertion of
  physical force so as to injure or abuse. A violent shaking.
  **Heb#:**5627 סרה / sa-rah *(noun)*: Turning aside—A
  change in location, position, station or residence, usually
  as a revolt.
  **Heb#:**7563 רשע / re-sha *(noun)*: Lost—Departed from
  the correct path or way, either out of ignorance or revolt.

**Grk#:**93 αδικια / ad-ee-kee-ah *(noun)*: Iniquity *Freq:* 25
  **Heb#:**5766 עול / ul *(noun)*: Wicked—A violation of right
  or duty.
  **Heb#:**5771 עוון / a-von *(noun)*: Iniquity—Gross injustice;
  wickedness. The result of twisted actions.

**Grk#:**125 Αιγυπτος / ah-ee-goop-tos *(name)*: Egypt *Freq:* 24
  **Heb#:**4714 מצרים / mits-ra-yim *(name)*: Mitsrayim—A
  place name of Hebrew origin meaning "Double trouble."

**Grk#:**129 αιμα / hah-ee-mah *(noun)*: Blood *Freq:* 99
**Heb#:**1818 דם / dam *(noun)*: Blood—The red fluid that circulates through the body.

**Grk#:**142 αιρω / ah-ee-ro *(verb)*: Take up *Freq:* 102
**Heb#:**5375 נסא / na-sa *(verb)*: Lift up—To lift up a burden or load and carry it; to lift up camp and begin a journey; to forgive in the sense of removing the offense.

**Grk#:**154 αιτεω / ahee-teh-o *(verb)*: Ask *Freq:* 71
**Heb#:**7592 שאל / sha-al *(verb)*: Enquire—To ask about; to search into; to seek to understand what is not known.

**Grk#:**165 αιων / ahee-ohn *(noun)*: Age *Freq:* 128
**Heb#:**5769 עולם / o-lam *(noun)*: Distant— A far off place as hidden beyond the horizon. A far off time as hidden from the present; the distant past or future. A place or time that cannot be perceived.

**Grk#:**166 αιωνιος / ahee-o-nee-os *(adj)*: Eternal *Freq:* 71
**Heb#:**5769 עולם / o-lam *(noun)*: Distant— A far off place as hidden beyond the horizon. A far off time as hidden from the present; the distant past or future. A place or time that cannot be perceived.

**Grk#:**169 ακαθαρτος / ak-ath-ar-tos *(adj)*: Unclean *Freq:* 30
**Heb#:**2931 טמא / ta-mey *(noun)*: Unclean—What is morally or physically impure; dirty, filthy.

**Grk#:189** ακοη / ak-o-ay *(noun)*: Hearing *Freq: 24*
**Heb#:8085** שמע / sha-ma *(verb)*: Hear—To perceive or apprehend by the ear; to listen to with attention. To obey.

**Grk#:190** ακολουθεω / ak-ol-oo-theh-o *(verb)*: Follow *Freq: 92*
**Heb#:1980** הלך / ha-lakh *(verb)*: Walk—To move along on foot; walk a journey; to go. Also, customs as a lifestyle that is walked or lived. {The Greek word ακολουθεω is a translation of this Hebrew word (הלך), but only when it is used in combination with the Hebrew word אחר (a'hhar, Strong's Heb. #310), meaning "after" - walk after.}

**Grk#:191** ακουω / ak-oo-o *(verb)*: Hear *Freq: 437*
**Heb#:8085** שמע / sha-ma *(verb)*: Hear—To perceive or apprehend by the ear; to listen to with attention. To obey.

**Grk#:225** αληθεια / al-ay-thi-a *(noun)*: Truth *Freq: 110*
**Heb#:571** אמת / e-met *(noun)*: Truth—The state of being the case. Fact. What is firm. Accurately so.

**Grk#:227** αληθης / al-ay-thace *(adj)*: True *Freq: 25*
**Heb#:571** אמת / e-met *(noun)*: Truth—The state of being the case. Fact. What is firm. Accurately so.

**Grk#:228** αληθινος / al-ay-thee-nos *(adj)*: True *Freq: 27*
**Heb#:571** אמת / e-met *(noun)*: Truth—The state of being the case. Fact. What is firm. Accurately so.

21

**Grk#:**230 αληθως / al-ay-thoce *(adv)*: Truly *Freq:* 21
    **Heb#:**546 אמנה / am-nah *(noun)*: Sure—Safe from danger or harm; marked by or given to feelings of confident certainty. What is firm.

**Grk#:**243 αλλος / al-los *(adj)*: Other *Freq:* 160
    **Heb#:**312 אחר / a-hhar *(noun)*: Other—One that remains or follows after another.

**Grk#:**264 αμαρτανω / ham-ar-tan-o *(verb)*: Sin *Freq:* 43
    **Heb#:**2398 חטא / hha-ta *(verb)*: Err—To miss the target, whether a literal target or a goal that is aimed for.

**Grk#:**266 αμαρτια / ham-ar-tee-ah *(noun)*: Sin *Freq:* 174
    **Heb#:**2403 חטאה / hha-ta-a *(noun)*: Error—An act or condition of ignorant or imprudent deviation from a code of behavior. A missing of the target in the sense of making a mistake. The sacrifice, which by transference, becomes the sin.

**Grk#:**268 αμαρτωλος / ham-ar-to-los *(adj)*: Sinner *Freq:* 47
    **Heb#:**2398 חטא / hha-ta *(verb)*: Err—To miss the target, whether a literal target or a goal that is aimed for. {The Greek word αμαρτωλος is a translation of the participle form of the Hebrew verb חטא meaning "one who errs."}

**Grk#:**281 αμην / am-ane *(noun)*: Amen *Freq:* 152
    **Heb#:**543 אמן / a-meyn *(noun)*: So be it—An affirmation of firmness and support.

**Grk#:**290 αμπελων / am-pel-ohn *(noun):* Vineyard *Freq:* 23
**Heb#:**3754 כרם / ke-rem *(noun):* Vineyard—A planting of grapevines.

**Grk#:**305 αναβαινω / an-ab-ah-ee-no *(verb):* Go up *Freq:* 82
**Heb#:**5927 עלה / a-lah *(verb):* Go up—To go, come or bring higher.

**Grk#:**314 αναγινωσκω / an-ag-in-oce-ko *(verb):* Read *Freq:* 33
**Heb#:**7121 קרא / qa-ra *(verb):* Call out—To raise one's voice or speak loudly and with urgency; to give a name; to meet in the sense of being called to a meeting; to have an encounter by chance; to read out loud in the sense of calling out words.

**Grk#:**321 αναγω / an-ag-o *(verb):* Bring *Freq:* 24
**Heb#:**935 בוא / bo *(verb):* Come—To move toward something; approach; enter. This can be understood as to come or to go. {The Greek word αναγω is a translation of the hiphil (causative) form of the Hebrew verb בוא meaning "to make come," or "bring."}

**Grk#:**337 αναιρεω / an-ahee-reh-o *(verb):* Kill *Freq:* 23
**Heb#:**2026 הרג / ha-rag *(verb):* Kill—To deprive of life; to slaughter.
**Heb#:**4191 מות / mut *(verb):* Die—To pass from physical life; to pass out of existence; to come to an end through death. {The Greek word αναιρεω is a translation of the hiphil (causative) form of the Hebrew verb מות meaning "make die" or "kill."}

**Grk#:386** αναστασις / an-as-tas-is *(noun)*: Resurrection *Freq:* 42

**Heb#:6965** קום / qum *(verb)*: Rise—To assume an upright position; to raise or rise up; to continue or establish.

**Grk#:406** Ανδρεας / an-dreh-as *(name)*: Andrew *Freq:* 13

**Heb#:None** אנדרי / an-drai *(name)*: Andrai—A Hebrew transliteration of a personal name of Greek origin meaning "Manly." {Many Hebrew names in the Greek New Testament are transliterated into Greek, such as we see with the Hebrew name שמעון (shimon), which is translitered into Greek as Σιμων (Simon), as well as a Greek name, such as the Greek name Πετρος (Petros) being used for Shimon (see Matthew 4:18). In the case of "Andrew" we are given his Greek name, but not his Hebrew name.}

**Grk#:417** ανεμος / an-em-os *(noun)*: Wind *Freq:* 31

**Heb#:7307** רוח / ru-ahh *(noun)*: Wind—A natural movement of air; breath. The breath of man, animal or God. The character. A space in between.

**Grk#:435** ανηρ / an-ayr *(noun)*: Man *Freq:* 215

**Heb#:120** אדם / a-dam *(noun)*: Human—Of, relating to, or characteristic of man. The first man. All of mankind as the descendants of the first man.

**Heb#:376** איש / ish *(noun)*: Man—An adult male human. As mortal. Also, used to mean "each" in the sense of an individual.

**Grk#:444** ανθρωπος / anth-ro-pos *(noun)*: Human *Freq:* 559
**Heb#:120** אדם / a-dam *(noun)*: Human—Of, relating to, or characteristic of man. The first man. All of mankind as the descendants of the first man.
**Heb#:376** איש / ish *(noun)*: Man—An adult male human. As mortal. Also, used to mean "each" in the sense of an individual.

**Grk#:450** ανιστημι / an-is-tay-mee *(verb)*: Arise *Freq:* 112
**Heb#:6965** קום / qum *(verb)*: Rise—To assume an upright position; to raise or rise up; to continue or establish.

**Grk#:455** ανοιγω / an-oy-go *(verb)*: Open *Freq:* 77
**Heb#:6605** פתח / pa-tahh *(verb)*: Open—To open up as opening a gate or door; to have no confining barrier.

**Grk#:490** Αντιοχεια / an-tee-okh-i-ah *(name)*: Antioch *Freq:* 18
**Heb#:None** אנטיוכיא / an-ti-okh-ya *(name)*: Anti'okh'ya—A Hebrew transliteration of a personal and place name, possibly of Syrian origin meaning "Driven against."

**Grk#:518** απαγγελλω / ap-ang-el-lo *(verb)*: Tell *Freq:* 45
**Heb#:5046** נגד / na-gad *(verb)*: Be face to face—To face another. {The Greek word απαγγελλω is a translation of the hiphil (causative) form of the Hebrew verb נגד meaning "tell" through the idea of making another come face to face.}

**Grk#:565** απερχομαι / ap-erkh-om-ahee *(verb)*: Go away *Freq:* 120

    **Heb#:935** בוא / bo *(verb)*: Come—To move toward something; approach; enter. This can be understood as to come or to go.

**Grk#:571** απιστος / ap-is-tos *(adj)*: Faithless *Freq:* 23

    **Heb#:539** אמן / a-man *(verb)*: Secure—Solidly fixed in place; to stand firm in the sense of a support. Not subject to change or revision. {The Greek word απιστος is a translation of the participle form of the Hebrew word אמן and is preceded by the word אין (ain, strong's Heb. #369), meaning "not" - "not a secure one."}

**Grk#:591** αποδιδωμι / ap-od-eed-o-mee *(verb)*: Pay *Freq:* 48

    **Heb#:7725** שוב / shuv *(verb)*: Turn back—To return to a previous place or state. {The Greek word αποδιδωμι is a combination of two Greek words: απο (apo), meaning "from" and διδωμι (didomi), meaning "give" (see Grk #1325 below for διδωμι (didomi). This Greek word αποδιδωμι is a translation of the hiphil (causative) form of the Hebrew verb שוב.}

    **Heb#:7999** שלם / sha-lam *(verb)*: Make restitution—To restore or make right through action, payment or restoration to a rightful owner.

**Grk#:599** αποθνησκω / ap-oth-nace-ko *(verb)*: Die *Freq:* 112

    **Heb#:4191** מות / mut *(verb)*: Die—To pass from physical life; to pass out of existence; to come to an end through death.

**Grk#:601** αποκαλυπτω / ap-ok-al-oop-to *(verb)*: Reveal *Freq:* 26
    **Heb#:1540** גלה / ga-lah *(verb)*: Remove the cover—To reveal something by exposing it. Usually to be exposed by the removal of clothing.

**Grk#:611** αποκρινομαι / ap-ok-ree-nom-ahee *(verb)*: Answer *Freq:* 250
    **Heb#:6030** ענה / a-nah *(verb)*: Answer—Something written or spoken in reply to a question.

**Grk#:615** αποκτεινω / ap-ok-ti-no *(verb)*: Kill *Freq:* 75
    **Heb#:2026** הרג / ha-rag *(verb)*: Kill—To deprive of life; to slaughter.
    **Heb#:4191** מות / mut *(verb)*: Die—To pass from physical life; to pass out of existence; to come to an end through death. {The Greek word αποκτεινω is a translation of the hiphil (causative) form of the Hebrew verb מות meaning "make die" or "kill."}

**Grk#:622** απολλυμι / ap-ol-loo-mee *(verb)*: Destroy/Perish *Freq:* 92
    **Heb#:6** אבד / a-vad *(verb)*: Perish—To be separated from the whole, life or functionality.

**Grk#:630** απολυω / ap-ol-oo-o *(verb)*: Release *Freq:* 69
    **Heb#:7971** שלח / sha-lahh *(verb)*: Send—To cause to go; to direct, order, or request to go.

**Grk#:649** αποστελλω / ap-os-tel-lo *(verb)*: Send *Freq:* 133
    **Heb#:7971** שלח / sha-lahh *(verb)*: Send—To cause to go; to direct, order, or request to go.

**Grk#:**652 αποστολος / ap-os-tol-os *(noun)*: Apostle *Freq:* 81
    **Heb#:**7971 שלח / sha-lahh *(verb)*: Send—To cause to go; to direct, order, or request to go. {The Greek word αποστολος is a translation of the participle form of the Hebrew verb שלח meaning "one who is sent."}

**Grk#:**680 απτομαι / hap-tom-ahee *(verb)*: Touch *Freq:* 36
    **Heb#:**5060 נגע / na-ga *(verb)*: Touch—To lay hands upon; to touch or strike; to be touched by a plague.

**Grk#:**721 αρνιον / ar-nee-on *(noun)*: Lamb *Freq:* 30
    **Heb#:**3532 כשב / ke-sev *(noun)*: Sheep—A mammal related to the goat domesticated for its flesh and wool.

**Grk#:**740 αρτος / ar-tos *(noun)*: Bread *Freq:* 99
    **Heb#:**3899 לחם / le-hhem *(noun)*: Bread—Baked and leavened food primarily made of flour or meal. Also food in general.

**Grk#:**746 αρχη / ar-khay *(noun)*: Beginning/Leader *Freq:* 58
    **Heb#:**7225 ראשית / rey-shit *(noun)*: Summit—The head, top or beginning of a place, such as a river or mountain, or a time, such as an event. The point at which something starts; origin, source.

**Grk#:**749 αρχιερευς / ar-khee-er-yuce *(noun)*: High priest *Freq:* 123
    **Heb#:**3548 כוהן / ko-heyn *(noun)*: Administrator—One who manages the affairs and activities of an organization. The administrators (often translated as "priest") of Israel are Levites who manage the Tent of Meeting, and later the Temple, as well as teach the people the teachings and

directions of Yahweh, and perform other duties, such as the inspection of people and structures for disease. {The Greek word αρχιερευς is a translation of the Hebrew verb כוהן when it is followed by the word גדול (gadol, Strong's Heb. #1419), meaning "great"- "great administrator."}

**Grk#:756** αρχομαι / ar-khom-ahee *(verb)*: Begin *Freq:* 84
**Heb#:2490** חלל / hha-lal *(verb)*: Pierce—To run into or through as with a pointed weapon or tool; pierce a hole through. {The Greek word αρχομαι is a translation of the hiphil (causative) form of the Hebrew verb חלל meaning "begin" through the idea of making a piercing into.}

**Grk#:758** αρχων / ar-khone *(noun)*: Ruler *Freq:* 37
**Heb#:4428** מלך / me-lekh *(noun)*: King—The male ruler of a nation or city state.
**Heb#:5387** נשיא / na-si *(noun)*: Captain—A military leader; the commander of a unit or a body of troops. The leader of a family, tribe or people as one who carries the burdens of the people.
**Heb#:7218** ראש / rosh *(noun)*: Head—The top of the body. A person in authority or role of leader. The top, beginning or first of something.
**Heb#:8269** שר / sar (noun): Noble—Possessing outstanding qualities or properties. Of high birth or exalted rank. One who has authority. May also mean "heavy" from the weight of responsibility on one in authority.

**Grk#:**769 ασθενεια / as-then-i-ah *(noun)*: Infirmity *Freq:* 24
    **Heb#:**6094 עצבת / a-tse-vet *(noun)*: Suffering—from sorrow or wound.

**Grk#:**770 ασθενεω / as-then-eh-o *(verb)*: Be weak *Freq:* 36
    **Heb#:**2470 חלה / hha-lah *(verb)*: Be sick—To be twisted through pain.

**Grk#:**772 ασθενης / as-then-ace *(adj)*: Weak *Freq:* 25
    **Heb#:**6041 עני / a-ni *(noun)*: Affliction—The cause of persistent suffering, pain or distress.
    **Heb#:**7504 רפה / ra-phah *(noun)*: Weak—Slack in body or mind.

**Grk#:**773 Ασια / as-ee-ah *(name)*: Asia *Freq:* 19
    **Heb#:**None אסיא / as-ya *(name)*: Asya—A Hebrew transliteration of a place name of unknown origin meaning "Orient."

**Grk#:**792 αστηρ / as-tare *(noun)*: Star *Freq:* 24
    **Heb#:**3556 כוכב / ko-khav *(noun)*: Star—A natural luminous body visible in the night sky.

**Grk#:**837 αυξανω / owx-an-o *(verb)*: Grow *Freq:* 22
    **Heb#:**6509 פרה / pa-rah *(verb)*: Reproduce—To produce new individuals of the same kind; to be abundant in fruit.

**Grk#:**863 αφιημι / af-ee-ay-mee *(verb)*: Leave *Freq:* 146
    **Heb#:**5375 נסא / na-sa *(verb)*: Lift up—To lift up a burden or load and carry it; to lift up camp and begin a journey; to forgive in the sense of removing the offense.

**Heb#:**5414 נתן / na-tan *(verb)*: Give—To make a present; to present a gift; to grant, allow or bestow by formal action.

**Heb#:**5545 סלח / sa-lahh *(verb)*: Forgive—To pardon; to overlook an offense and treat the offender as not guilty.

**Heb#:**5800 עזב / a-zav (verb): Leave—To go away from; to neglect.

**Grk#:**897 Βαβυλων / bab-oo-lone *(name)*: Babylon *Freq:* 12

    **Heb#:**894 בבל / ba-vel *(name)*: Bavel—A place name of Hebrew origin meaning "Mixed."

**Grk#:**906 βαλλω / bal-lo *(verb)*: Cast *Freq:* 125

    **Heb#:**3384 ירה / ya-rah *(verb)*: Throw—To propel through the air by a forward motion; to drizzle as a throwing down of water; to teach in the sense of throwing or pointing a finger in a straight line as the direction one is to walk.

    **Heb#:**7993 שלך / sha-lakh *(verb)*: Throw out—To remove from a place, usually in a sudden or unexpected manner; to cast out, down or away.

**Grk#:**907 βαπτιζω / bap-tid-zo *(verb)*: Baptize *Freq:* 80

    **Heb#:**2881 טבל / ta-val *(verb)*: Dip—To plunge or immerse momentarily or partially, as under the surface of a liquid, to moisten, cool, or coat.

    **Heb#:**7364 רחץ / ra-hhats *(verb)*: Bathe—To cleanse by being immersed in, or washing with, water.

**Grk#:908** βαπτισμα / bap-tis-mah *(noun)*: Baptism *Freq:* 22
**Heb#:2881** טבל / ta-val *(verb)*: Dip—To plunge or immerse momentarily or partially, as under the surface of a liquid, to moisten, cool, or coat.
**Heb#:7364** רחץ / ra-hhats *(verb)*: Bathe—To cleanse by being immersed in, or washing with, water.

**Grk#:921** βαρναβας / bar-nab-as *(name)*: Barnabas *Freq:* 29
**Heb#:None** בר-נבא / bar na-va *(name)*: Bar Nava—A personal name of Aramaic origin meaning "son of a prophet."

**Grk#:932** βασιλεια / bas-il-i-ah *(noun)*: Kingdom *Freq:* 162
**Heb#:4438** מלכות / mal-kut *(noun)*: Empire—The area under the control of a king; a kingdom.

**Grk#:935** βασιλευς / bas-il-yooce *(noun)*: King *Freq:* 118
**Heb#:4428** מלך / me-lekh *(noun)*: King—The male ruler of a nation or city state.

**Grk#:936** βασιλευω / bas-il-yoo-o *(verb)*: Reign *Freq:* 21
**Heb#:4427** מלך / ma-lakh *(verb)*: Reign—To rule over a kingdom as king or queen.

**Grk#:941** βασταζω / bas-tad-zo *(verb)*: Bear *Freq:* 27
**Heb#:5375** נסא / na-sa *(verb)*: Lift up—To lift up a burden or load and carry it; to lift up camp and begin a journey; to forgive in the sense of removing the offense.

**Grk#:**975 βιβλιον / bib-lee-on *(noun)*: Book *Freq:* 32
    **Heb#:**5612 סיפרה / siph-rah *(noun)*: Scroll—A document or record written on a sheet of papyrus, leather or parchment and rolled up for storage.

**Grk#:**987 βλασφημεω / blas-fay-meh-o *(verb)*: Blaspheme *Freq:* 35
    **Heb#:**1442 גדף / ga-daph *(verb)*: Taunt—To reproach in a sarcastic, insulting, or jeering manner.
    **Heb#:**2778 חרף / hha-raph *(verb)*: Taunt—To pierce another with sharp words of reproach or scorn. (see Psalms 42:10). A nose ring is put in the piercing of the nose as a sign of betrothal (see Genesis 24:47).
    **Heb#:**5006 נאץ / na-ats *(verb)*: Despise—To regard with contempt, distaste, disgust, or disdain.

**Grk#:**991 βλεπω / blep-o *(verb)*: See *Freq:* 135
    **Heb#:**7200 ראה / ra-ah *(verb)*: See—To take notice; to perceive something or someone; to see visions.

**Grk#:**1056 Γαλιλαια / gal-il-ah-yah *(name)*: Galilee *Freq:* 63
    **Heb#:**1551 גליל / ga-lil *(name)*: galiyl—A place name of Hebrew origin meaning "Ring."

**Grk#:**1060 γαμεω / gam-eh-o *(verb)*: Marry *Freq:* 29
    **Heb#:**1166 בעל / ba-al *(verb)*: Marry—To join as husband and wife.

**Grk#:**1074 γενεα / ghen-eh-ah *(noun)*: Generation *Freq:* 42
    **Heb#:**1755 דור / dor *(noun)*: Generation—A body of living beings constituting a single step in the line of descent from an ancestor.

**Grk#:**1080 γενναω / ghen-nah-o *(verb)*: Begat *Freq:* 97
**Heb#:**3205 ילד / ya-lad *(verb)*: Bring forth—To issue out; to bring forth children, either by the woman who bears them or the man who fathers them.

**Grk#:**1093 γη / ghay *(noun)*: Earth *Freq:* 252
**Heb#:**776 ארץ / e-rets *(noun)*: Land—The solid part of the earth's surface. The whole of the earth or a region.

**Grk#:**1085 γενος / ghen-os *(noun)*: Kind *Freq:* 21
**Heb#:**4327 מן / min *(noun)*: Kind—A category of creature that comes from its own kind as a firm rule.

**Grk#:**1097 γινωσκω / ghin-oce-ko *(verb)*: Know *Freq:* 223
**Heb#:**3045 ידע / ya-da *(verb)*: Know—To have an intimate and personal understanding; to have an intimate relationship with another person, usually sexual.

**Grk#:**1100 γλωσσα / gloce-sah *(noun)*: Tongue *Freq:* 50
**Heb#:**3956 לשון / la-shon *(noun)*: Tongue—A fleshy moveable appendage on the floor of the mouth used in speaking and eating. Also, language as a tongue.

**Grk#:**1107 γνωριζω / gno-rid-zo *(verb)*: Make known *Freq:* 24
**Heb#:**3045 ידע / ya-da *(verb)*: Know—To have an intimate and personal understanding; to have an intimate relationship with another person, usually sexual. {The Greek word γνωριζω is a translation of the hiphil (causative) form of the Hebrew verb ידע meaning "make known."}

# New Testament Greek to Hebrew Dictionary

**Grk#:**1108 γνωσις / gno-sis *(noun)*: Knowledge *Freq:* 29
**Heb#:**1844 דעה / dey-ah *(noun)*: Comprehension—An intimacy with a person, idea or concept.
**Heb#:**1847 דעת / da-at *(noun)*: Discernment—The quality of being able to grasp and comprehend what is obscure. An intimacy with a person, idea or concept. Knowledge

**Grk#:**1122 γραμματευς / gram-mat-yooce *(noun)*: Scribe *Freq:* 67
**Heb#:**5608 ספר / sa-phar *(verb)*: Count— To find the total number of units. Also to give an account on record. {The Greek word γραμματευς is a translation of the piel (intensive) participle form of the Hebrew verb ספר meaning "one who recounts," as one who records an accounting.}

**Grk#:**1124 γραφη / graf-ay *(noun)*: Scripture *Freq:* 51
**Heb#:**3791 כתב / k-tav *(noun)*: Writing—A record of a story, thoughts or instructions inscribed on a variety of media including stone, papyrus, leather or parchment.

**Grk#:**1125 γραφω / graf-o *(verb)*: Write *Freq:* 209
**Heb#:**3789 כתב / ka-tav *(verb)*: Write—To inscribe a story, thoughts or instructions on a variety of media including stone, papyrus, leather or parchment.

**Grk#:**1127 γρηγορεω / gray-go-re-o *(verb)*: Watch *Freq:* 23
**Heb#:**8104 שמר / sha-mar *(verb)*: Safeguard—The act or the duty of protecting or defending; to watch over or guard in the sense of preserving or protecting.
**Heb#:**6822 צפה / tsa-phah *(verb)*: Keep watch—To be on the look-out for danger or opportunity.

**Grk#:**1135 γυνη / goo-nay *(noun)*: Woman *Freq:* 221
    **Heb#:**802 אִישָׁה / i-shah *(noun)*: Woman—An adult female person. As mortal.

**Grk#:**1138 Δαυιδ / dau-eed *(name)*: David *Freq:* 59
    **Heb#:**1732 דּוִיד / da-vid *(name)*: Daviyd—A personal name of Hebrew origin meaning "Beloved."

**Grk#:**1140 δαιμονιον / dahee-mon-ee-on *(noun)*: Demon *Freq:* 60
    **Heb#:**457 אֱלִיל / e-lil *(noun)*: Worthless—A god or being without power.
    **Heb#:**6728 צִיִי / tsi-i *(noun)*: Desert—A dry and arid region usually void of water and vegetation.
    **Heb#:**7700 שֵׁד / shad *(noun)*: Breast—Milk-producing glandular organs situated on the chest in the female; the fore part of the body between the neck and the abdomen. Also a goat-idol from the teats of the goat.
    **Heb#:**8163 שָׂעִיר / sa-ir (noun): Goat—Related to the sheep but of lighter build and with backwardly arching horns, a short tail, and usually straight hair.

**Grk#:**1154 Δαμασκος / dam-as-kos *(name)*: Damascus *Freq:* 15
    **Heb#:**1834 דַּמֶּסֶק / dam-seq *(name)*: Damseq—A place name of Hebrew origin meaning "Blood of Sackcloth."

**Grk#:**1166 δεικνυω / dike-noo-o *(verb)*: Show *Freq:* 31
    **Heb#:**3384 יָרָה / ya-rah *(verb)*: Throw—To propel through the air by a forward motion; to drizzle as a throwing down of water; to teach in the sense of throwing or pointing a finger in a straight line as the direction one is to walk.

**Heb#:**7200 ראה / ra-ah *(verb)*: See—To take notice; to perceive something or someone; to see visions. {The Greek word δεικνυω is a translation of the hiphil (causative) form of the Hebrew verb ראה meaning "make see" or "show."}

**Grk#:**1176 δεκα / dek-ah *(noun)*: Ten *Freq: 27*
**Heb#:**6235 עשר / e-ser *(noun)*: Ten—A cardinal number.

**Grk#:**1186 δενδρον / den-dron *(noun)*: Tree *Freq: 26*
**Heb#:**6086 עץ / eyts *(noun)*: Tree—A woody perennial plant with a supporting stem or trunk and multiple branches. Meaning "wood" when written in the plural form.

**Grk#:**1188 δεξιος / dex-ee-os *(adj)*: Right *Freq: 53*
**Heb#:**3225 ימין / ya-min *(noun)*: Right hand—The hand on the right side of a person. Also, a direction as in "to the right."

**Grk#:**1189 δεομαι / deh-om-ahee *(verb)*: Request *Freq: 22*
**Heb#:**4994 נא / na *(noun)*: Please—A pleading or request for action from another.

**Grk#:**1208 δευτερος / dyoo-ter-os *(adj)*: Second *Freq: 47*
**Heb#:**8145 שני / shey-ni *(noun)*: Second—An ordinal number.

**Grk#:**1209 δεχομαι / dekh-om-ahee *(verb)*: Receive *Freq: 59*
**Heb#:**3947 לקח / la-qahh *(verb)*: Take—To receive what is given; to gain possession by seizing.

**Heb#:6901** קבל / qa-val *(verb)*: Receive—To take or accept what has been given.

**Grk#:1210** δεω / deh-o *(verb)*: Bind *Freq:* 44
**Heb#:631** אסר / a-sar *(verb)*: Tie up—To wrap or fasten with a cord.

**Grk#:1228** διαβολος / dee-ab-ol-os *(adj)*: Devil *Freq:* 38
**Heb#:7854** סטן / sa-tan *(noun)*: Opponent—One who is on the opposing side of an action or thought; an adversary.

**Grk#:1242** διαθηκη / dee-ath-ay-kay *(noun)*: Covenant *Freq:* 33
**Heb#:1285** ברית / be-rit *(noun)*: Covenant—A solemn and binding agreement between two or more parties especially for the performance of some action. Often instituted through a sacrifice.

**Grk#:1247** διακονεω / dee-ak-on-eh-o *(verb)*: Minister *Freq:* 37
**Heb#:5647** עבד / a-vad *(verb)*: Serve—To provide a service to another, as a servant or slave or to work at a profession.
**Heb#:8334** שרת / sha-rat *(verb)*: Minister—To give aid or service; to be in service to another.

**Grk#:1248** διακονια / dee-ak-on-ee-ah *(noun)*: Ministry *Freq:* 34
**Heb#:5656** עבודה / a-vo-dah *(noun)*: Service—Labor provided by a servant or slave.

**Grk#:**1249 διακονος / dee-ak-on-os *(noun)*: Minister *Freq:* 31
> **Heb#:**5650 עבד / e-ved *(noun)*: Servant—One who provides a service to another, as a slave, bondservant or hired hand.

**Grk#:**1319 διδασκαλια / did-as-kal-ee-ah *(noun)*: Doctrine *Freq:* 21
> **Heb#:**3948 לקח / la-qahh *(noun)*: Learning— Teachings and instructions that are received in the sense of being taken.
>
> **Heb#:**8451 תורה / to-rah *(noun)*: Teaching—Acquired knowledge or skills that mark the direction one is to take in life. A straight direction. Knowledge passed from one person to another.

**Grk#:**1320 διδασκαλος / did-as-kal-os *(noun)*: Teacher *Freq:* 58
> **Heb#:**3925 למד / la-mad *(verb)*: Learn—To acquire knowledge or skill through instruction from one who is experienced. {The Greek word διδασκαλος is a translation of the piel (intensive) participle form of the Hebrew verb למד meaning "one who causes to learn," or a "teacher."}
>
> **Heb#:**4175 מורה / mo-reh *(noun)*: Pointing—A rain through the sense of rain clouds in the distance that point one to water and green grasses. Also a teacher as one who points out the way one is to go.

**Grk#:**1321 διδασκω / did-as-ko *(verb)*: Teach *Freq:* 97
> **Heb#:**3384 ירה / ya-rah *(verb)*: Throw—To propel through the air by a forward motion; to throw down rain that when seen from a distance points to water; to teach

in the sense of throwing or pointing a finger in a straight line as the direction one is to walk.

**Heb#:3925** למד / la-mad *(verb)*: Learn—To acquire knowledge or skill through instruction from one who is experienced. {The Greek word διδασκω is a translation of the piel (intensive) form of the Hebrew verb למד meaning "cause to learn," or "teach."}

**Grk#:1322** διδαχη / did-akh-ay *(noun)*: Teaching *Freq:* 30

**Heb#:3948** לקח / le-qahh *(noun)*: Learning—Teachings and instructions that are received in the sense of being taken.

**Heb#:8451** תורה / to-rah *(noun)*: Teaching—Acquired knowledge or skills that mark the direction one is to take in life. A straight direction. Knowledge passed from one person to another.

**Grk#:1325** διδωμι / did-o-mee *(verb)*: Give *Freq:* 413

**Heb#:5414** נתן / na-tan *(verb)*: Give—To make a present; to present a gift; to grant, allow or bestow by formal action.

**Grk#:1330** διερχομαι / dee-er-khom-ahee *(verb)*: Pass *Freq:* 43

**Heb#:1980** הלך / ha-lakh *(verb)*: Walk—To move along on foot; walk a journey; to go. Also, customs as a lifestyle that is walked or lived.

**Grk#:1342** δικαιος / dik-ah-yos *(adj)*: Righteous *Freq:* 81

**Heb#:6662** צדיק / tsa-diyq *(noun)*: Steadfast—One that makes or sets right. Conforming to fact, standard or truth.

**Heb#:6664** צדק / tse-deq *(noun)*: Steadfast—The following of the established path or course of action.

**Grk#:1343** δικαιοσυνη / dik-ah-yos-oo-nay *(noun)*: Righteousness *Freq:* 92
>   **Heb#:6664** צדק / tse-deq *(noun)*: Steadfast—The following of the established path or course of action.
>   **Heb#:6666** צדקה / tse-de-qah *(noun)*: Steadfastness—Conformity to fact, standard or truth.

**Grk#:1344** δικαιοω / dik-ah-yo-o *(verb)*: Justify *Freq:* 40
>   **Heb#:6663** צדק / tsa-daq *(verb)*: Be steadfast—To walk on the right path without losing the way.

**Grk#:1377** διωκω / dee-o-ko *(verb)*: Persecute *Freq:* 44
>   **Heb#:7291** רדף / ra-daph *(verb)*: Pursue—To follow in order to overtake, capture, kill, or defeat; to pursue in chase or persecution.
>   **Heb#:7323** רוץ / ruts *(verb)*: Run—To go faster than a walk.

**Grk#:1380** δοκεω / dok-eh-o *(verb)*: Think *Freq:* 63
>   **Heb#:2803** חשב / hha-shav *(verb)*: Think—To plan or design a course of action, item or invention.

**Grk#:1381** δοκιμαζω / dok-im-ad-zo *(verb)*: Prove *Freq:* 23
>   **Heb#:974** בחן / ba-hhan *(verb)*: Examine—To inspect closely; to test, try or scrutinize.

**Grk#:1391** δοξα / dox-ah *(noun)*: Glory *Freq:* 168
>   **Heb#:3519** כבוד / ka-vod *(noun)*: Armament—The arms and equipment of a soldier or military unit. From a root meaning "heavy" and often paralleled with other weapons. Figurative for power.

**Grk#:**1392 δοξαζω / dox-ad-zo *(verb)*: Glorify *Freq:* 62
**Heb#:**3513 כבד / ka-vad *(verb)*: Be heavy—To be great in weight, wealth or importance.

**Grk#:**1398 δουλευω / dool-yoo-o *(verb)*: Serve *Freq:* 25
**Heb#:**5647 עבד / a-vad *(verb)*: Serve—To provide a service to another, as a servant or slave or to work at a profession.

**Grk#:**1401 δουλος / doo-los *(adj)*: Servant *Freq:* 125
**Heb#:**5650 עבד / e-ved *(noun)*: Servant—One who provides a service to another, as a slave, bondservant or hired hand.

**Grk#:**1410 δυναμαι / doo-nam-ahee *(verb)*: Can *Freq:* 210
**Heb#:**3201 יכל / ya-khal *(verb)*: Be able—To successfully prevail, overcome or endure.

**Grk#:**1411 δυναμις / doo-nam-is *(noun)*: Power *Freq:* 120
**Heb#:**410 אל / el *(noun)*: Mighty one—One who holds authority over others, such as a judge, chief or god. In the sense of being yoked to one another.
**Heb#:**3581 כוח / ko-ahh *(noun)*: Strength—The quality or state of being strong.
**Heb#:**5797 עוז / oz *(noun)*: Boldness—Knowing one's position or authority and standing in it. Strengthened and protected from danger.

**Grk#:**1415 δυνατος / doo-nat-os *(adj)*: Possible *Freq:* 35
**Heb#:**1368 גיבור / gi-bor *(noun)*: Courageous—Having or characterized by mental or moral strength to venture, persevere, and withstand danger, fear or difficulty.

**Heb#:**2428 חיל / hha-yil *(noun)*: Force—The pressure exerted to make a piercing.

**Heb#:**3201 יכל / ya-khal *(verb)*: Be able—To successfully prevail, overcome or endure.

**Grk#:**1417 δυο / doo-o *(noun)*: Two *Freq:* 135
   **Heb#:**8147 שנים / she-na-yim *(noun)*: Two—A cardinal number.

**Grk#:**1448 εγγιζω / eng-id-zo *(verb)*: Draw nigh *Freq:* 43
   **Heb#:**5066 נגש / na-gash *(verb)*: Draw near—To bring close to another.
   **Heb#:**7126 קרב / qa-rav *(verb)*: Come near—To come close by or near to.

**Grk#:**1451 εγγυς / eng-goos *(adv)*: At hand *Freq:* 30
   **Heb#:**7138 קרוב / qa-rov *(noun)*: Near—Close to; at or within a short distance from. Also, a kin, as a near relative.

**Grk#:**1453 εγειρω / eg-i-ro *(verb)*: Rise *Freq:* 141
   **Heb#:**6965 קום / qum *(verb)*: Rise—To assume an upright position; to raise or rise up; to continue or establish.
   **Heb#:**7311 רום / rum *(verb)*: Raise—To lift something up.

**Grk#:**1484 εθνος / eth-nos *(noun)*: Gentile *Freq:* 164
   **Heb#:**1471 גוי / goy *(noun)*: Nation—An area surrounded by borders and inhabited by a people of a common ancestor or origin.

**Grk#:**1504 εικων / i-kone *(noun):* Image *Freq:* 23
**Heb#:**1823 דמות / da-mut *(noun):* Likeness—Copy; resemblance. The quality or state of being like something or someone else.
**Heb#:**6754 צלם / tse-lem *(noun):* Image—A reproduction or imitation of the form of a person or thing. The form of something as a shadow of the original.

**Grk#:**1515 ειρηνη / i-ray-nay *(noun):* Peace *Freq:* 92
**Heb#:**7965 שלום / sha-lom *(noun):* Completeness—Something that has been finished or made whole. A state of being complete.

**Grk#:**1520 εις / hice *(noun):* One *Freq:* 271
**Heb#:**259 אחד / e-hhad *(noun):* Unit—A unit within the whole, a unified group. A single quantity.

**Grk#:**1525 εισερχομαι / ice-er-khom-ahee *(verb):* Enter *Freq:* 198
**Heb#:**935 בוא / bo *(verb):* Come—To move toward something; approach; enter. This can be understood as to come or to go.

**Grk#:**1544 εκβαλλω / ek-bal-lo *(verb):* Cast out *Freq:* 82
**Heb#:**1644 גרש / ga-rash *(verb):* Cast out—To drive out, expel, thrust away.

**Grk#:**1577 εκκλησια / ek-klay-see-ah *(noun):* Assembly *Freq:* 118
**Heb#:**6951 קהל / qa-hal *(noun):* Assembly—A large group, as a gathering of the flock of sheep to the shepherd.

# New Testament Greek to Hebrew Dictionary

**Grk#:1586** εκλεγομαι / ek-leg-om-ahee *(verb)*: Choose *Freq:* 21
 **Heb#:977** בחר / ba-hhar *(verb)*: Choose—To select freely and after consideration.

**Grk#:1588** εκλεκτος / ek-lek-tos *(adj)*: Chosen *Freq:* 23
 **Heb#:977** בחר / ba-hhar *(verb)*: Choose—To select freely and after consideration.
 **Heb#:4005** מבחר / miv-hhar *(noun)*: Chosen—One who is the object of choice or of divine favor.

**Grk#:1607** εκπορευομαι / ek-por-yoo-om-ahee *(verb)*: Proceed *Freq:* 35
 **Heb#:3318** יצא / ya-tsa *(verb)*: Go out—To go, come or issue forth.

**Grk#:1632** εκχεω / ek-kheh-o *(verb)*: Pour out *Freq:* 28
 **Heb#:8210** שפך / sha-phakh *(verb)*: Pour out—To let flow a liquid, often the blood of an animal in sacrifice or a man.

**Grk#:1653** ελεεω / el-eh-eh-o *(verb)*: Have mercy on *Freq:* 31
 **Heb#:2603** חנן / hha-nan *(verb)*: Show beauty—To give or show beauty, grace or mercy to another.

**Grk#:1656** ελεος / el-eh-os *(noun)*: Mercy *Freq:* 28
 **Heb#:2617** חסד / hhe-sed *(noun)*: Kindness—Of a sympathetic nature; quality or state of being sympathetic. In the sense of bowing the neck to another as a sign of kindness.

**Grk#:**1658 ελευθερος / el-yoo-ther-os *(adj)*: Free *Freq:* 23
**Heb#:**2670 חפשי / hhaph-shi *(noun)*: Free—Released from bondage or burden of obligation. Emancipation.

**Grk#:**1672 Ελλην / hel-lane *(name)*: Greek *Freq:* 27
**Heb#:**3120 יון / ya-van *(name)*: Yavan—A place name of Hebrew origin meaning "Wine" (from the Hebrew word יין-yayin, meaning wine) The Hebrew name for one from "Greece."

**Grk#:**1679 ελπιζω / el-pid-zo *(verb)*: Hope *Freq:* 32
**Heb#:**982 בטח / ba-tahh *(verb)*: Cling—To grab hold of someone or something that is secure and safe.

**Grk#:**1680 ελπις / el-pece *(noun)*: Hope *Freq:* 54
**Heb#:**8615 תקוה / tiq-vah *(noun)*: Waiting—A standing still in anticipation or expectation.

**Grk#:**1746 ενδυω / en-doo-o *(verb)*: Put on *Freq:* 29
**Heb#:**3847 לבש / la-vash *(verb)*: Wear—To cover with cloth or clothing; to provide with clothing; put on clothing. {The Greek word ενδυω is a translation of the hiphil (causative) form of the Hebrew verb לבש meaning "to make wear," or "clothe."}

**Grk#:**1754 ενεργεω / en-erg-eh-o *(verb)*: Work *Freq:* 21
**Heb#:**6466 פעל / pa-al *(verb)*: Make—To perform a task of physical labor.

**Grk#:**1785 εντολη / en-tol-ay *(noun)*: Commandment *Freq:* 71
**Heb#:**4687 מצוה / mits-vah *(noun)*: Directive—The direction to go. Serving or intended to guide, govern, or influence; serving to point direction.

**Grk#:**1831 εξερχομαι / ex-er-khom-ahee *(verb)*: Go out *Freq:* 222
**Heb#:**3318 יצא / ya-tsa *(verb)*: Go out—To go, come or issue forth.

**Grk#:**1832 εξεστι / ex-es-tee *(verb)*: Be lawful *Freq:* 32
**Heb#:**4941 משפט / mish-pat *(noun)*: Decision—A pronounced opinion.

**Grk#:**1849 εξουσια / ex-oo-see-ah *(noun)*: Power *Freq:* 103
**Heb#:**4475 ממשלה / mem-sha-lah *(noun)*: Regulation— An authoritative rule dealing with details or procedure. The power and authority of one to regulate and control over another.

**Grk#:**1859 εορτη / heh-or-tay *(noun)*: Feast *Freq:* 27
**Heb#:**2282 חג / hhag *(noun)*: Feast—A commemoration of a special event with dancing, rejoicing, and sharing of food. A ceremony of joy and thanksgiving. A festival with a magnificent meal which is shared with a number of guests.

**Grk#:**1860 επαγγελια / ep-ang-el-ee-ah *(noun)*: Promise *Freq:* 53
**Heb#:**1697 דבר / da-var *(noun)*: Word—An arrangement of words, ideas or concepts to form sentences. A promise in the sense of being "one's word." An action in the sense

of acting out an arrangement. A plague as an act. A matter or thing.

**Grk#:**1905 επερωταω / ep-er-o-tah-o *(verb)*: Ask *Freq:* 59
    **Heb#:**7592 שאל / sha-al *(verb)*: Enquire—To ask about; to search into; to seek to understand what is not known.

**Grk#:**1921 επιγινωσκω / ep-ig-in-oce-ko *(verb)*: Know *Freq:* 42
    **Heb#:**3045 ידע / ya-da *(verb)*: Know—To have an intimate and personal understanding; to have an intimate relationship with another person, usually sexual.

**Grk#:**1939 επιθυμια / ep-ee-thoo-mee-ah *(noun)*: Lust *Freq:* 38
    **Heb#:**183 אוה / a-vah *(verb)*: Yearn—To have an earnest or strong desire; long.
    **Heb#:**2530 חמד / hha-mad *(verb)*: Crave—To have a strong or inward desire for something.
    **Heb#:**8378 תאוה / ta-a-vah *(noun)*: Yearning—To long persistently, wistfully, or sadly. What is desired, whether good or bad.

**Grk#:**1941 επικαλεομαι / ep-ee-kal-eh-om-ahee *(verb)*: Call on *Freq:* 32
    **Heb#:**7121 קרא / qa-ra *(verb)*: Call out—To raise one's voice or speak loudly and with urgency; to give a name; to meet in the sense of being called to a meeting; to have an encounter by chance; to read out loud in the sense of calling out words.

**Grk#:**1992 επιστολη / ep-is-tol-ay *(noun)*: Letter *Freq:* 24
    **Heb#:**107 אגרת / i-ge-ret *(noun)*: Letter—A document or record written on a sheet of papyrus, leather or parchment and rolled up for storage.
    **Heb#:**3791 כתב / ke-tav *(noun)*: Writing— A record of a story, thoughts or instructions inscribed on a variety of mediums including stone, papyrus, leather or parchment.

**Grk#:**1994 επιστρεφω / ep-ee-stref-o *(verb)*: Turn *Freq:* 39
    **Heb#:**6437 פנה / pa-nah *(verb)*: Turn—To rotate or revolve; to face another direction; to turn the face; to turn directions; to turn something back or away.
    **Heb#:**7725 שוב / shuv *(verb)*: Turn back—To return to a previous place or state.

**Grk#:**2007 επιτιθημι / ep-ee-tith-ay-mee *(verb)*: Lay on *Freq:* 42
    **Heb#:**5414 נתן / na-tan *(verb)*: Give—To make a present; to present a gift; to grant, allow or bestow by formal action.
    **Heb#:**7760 שים / sim *(verb)*: Place—To put or set in a particular place, position, situation, or relation.

**Grk#:**2008 επιτιμαω / ep-ee-tee-mah-o *(verb)*: Rebuke *Freq:* 29
    **Heb#:**1605 גער / ga-ar *(verb)*: Rebuke—A communication directed toward a disorderly person to effect a return to their rightful place of order.

**Grk#:**2033 επτα / hep-tah *(noun)*: Seven *Freq:* 87
    **Heb#:**7651 שבע / she-va *(noun)*: Seven—A cardinal number.

**Grk#:**2036 επω / ep-o *(verb)*: Say *Freq:* 977
    **Heb#:**559 אמר / a-mar *(verb)*: Say—To speak chains of words that form sentences.
    **Heb#:**1696 דבר / da-var *(verb)*: Speak—To say a careful arrangement of words or commands.

**Grk#:**2038 εργαζομαι / er-gad-zom-ahee *(verb)*: Work *Freq:* 39
    **Heb#:**5647 עבד / a-vad *(verb)*: Serve—To provide a service to another, as a servant or slave or to work at a profession.
    **Heb#:**6466 פעל / pa-al *(verb)*: Make—To perform a task of physical labor.

**Grk#:**2041 εργον / er-gon *(noun)*: Work *Freq:* 176
    **Heb#:**4399 מלאכה / me-la-khah *(noun)*: Business—The principal occupation of one's life. A service.

**Grk#:**2046 ερεω / er-eh-o *(verb)*: Say *Freq:* 71
    **Heb#:**559 אמר / a-mar *(verb)*: Say—To speak chains of words that form sentences.

**Grk#:**2048 ερημος / er-ay-mos *(noun)*: Wilderness *Freq:* 50
    **Heb#:**4057 מדבר / mid-bar *(noun)*: Wilderness—A tract or region uncultivated and uninhabited by human beings. Place of order, a sanctuary.

**Grk#:**2064 ερχομαι / er-khom-ahee *(verb)*: Come *Freq:* 643
    **Heb#:**935 בוא / bo *(verb)*: Come—To move toward something; approach; enter. This can be understood as to come or to go.

**Grk#:**2065 ερωταω / er-o-tah-o *(verb)*: Ask *Freq:* 58
    **Heb#:**7592 שאל / sha-al *(verb)*: Enquire—To ask about; to search into; to seek to understand what is not known.

**Grk#:**2068 εσθιω / es-thee-o *(verb)*: Eat *Freq:* 65
    **Heb#:**398 אכל / a-khal *(verb)*: Eat—To consume food; to destroy. A devouring of a fire.

**Grk#:**2078 εσχατος / es-khat-os *(adj)*: Last *Freq:* 54
    **Heb#:**314 אחרון / a-hha-ron *(noun)*: Last—In, to or toward the back. To be in back of, at the rear or following after something.
    **Heb#:**319 אחרית / a-hha-rit *(noun)*: End—A final point that marks the extent of something. The latter time as coming after everything else.

**Grk#:**2087 ετερος / het-er-os *(adj)*: Other *Freq:* 99
    **Heb#:**312 אחר / a-hhar *(noun)*: Other— One that remains or follows after another.

**Grk#:**2090 ετοιμαζω / het-oy-mad-zo *(verb)*: Prepare *Freq:* 40
    **Heb#:**3559 כון / kun *(verb)*: Prepare—To put in proper condition or readiness.

**Grk#:**2094 ετος / et-os *(noun)*: Year *Freq:* 49
    **Heb#:**8141 שנה / sha-nah *(noun)*: Year—The period of approximately 365 solar days.

**Grk#:**2097 ευαγγελιζω / yoo-ang-ghel-id-zo *(verb)*: Preach *Freq:* 55

> **Heb#:**1319 בשר / ba-sar *(verb)*: Report—To provide good news, often followed by a feast where meat is prepared in celebration.

**Grk#:**2098 ευαγγελιον / yoo-ang-ghel-ee-on *(noun)*: Gospel *Freq:* 77

> **Heb#:**1309 בשורה / be-so-rah *(noun)*: Good news—A report of exciting information, often followed by a feast where meat is prepared in celebration.

**Grk#:**2127 ευλογεω / yoo-log-eh-o *(verb)*: Bless *Freq:* 44

> **Heb#:**1288 ברך / ba-rakh *(verb)*: Kneel—To bend the knee, to kneel in homage or to kneel down to get a drink of water. {The Greek word ευλογεω is a translation of the piel (intensive) form of the Hebrew verb ברך meaning "to kneel to another in respect," either literally or figuratively.}

**Grk#:**2147 ευρισκω / hyoo-ris-ko *(verb)*: Find *Freq:* 178

> **Heb#:**4672 מצא / ma-tsa *(verb)*: Find—To come upon, often accidentally; to meet with; to discover and secure through searching.

**Grk#:**2168 ευχαριστεω / yoo-khar-is-teh-o *(verb)*: Give thanks *Freq:* 39

> **Heb#:**3034 ידה / ya-dah *(verb)*: Throw the hand—To stretch out the hand to grab; to show praise or confession.

**Grk#:2181** Εφεσος / ef-es-os *(name)*: Ephesus *Freq:* 15
**Heb#:**None אפסוס / eph-sos *(name)*: Ephsos—A Hebrew transliteration of a place name of unknown origin meaning "Permitted."

**Grk#:2190** εχθρος / ech-thros *(adj)*: Enemy *Freq:* 32
**Heb#:**341 איב / a-yav *(verb)*: Attack—To be antagonistic or unfriendly to another. An action taken by an enemy. {The Greek word εχθρος is a translation of the participle form of the Hebrew verb איב meaning "one who attacks," an "enemy."}

**Grk#:2198** ζαω / dzah-o *(verb)*: Live *Freq:* 143
**Heb#:**2421 חיה / hhay-yah *(verb)*: Live—To be alive and continue alive. Have life within. The revival of life gained from food or other necessity.

**Grk#:2199** Ζεβεδαιος / dzeb-ed-ah-yos *(name)*: Zebedee *Freq:* 12
**Heb#:**None זבדי / zav-di *(name)*: Zavdiy—A personal name of Hebrew origin meaning "My gift."

**Grk#:2212** ζητεω / dzay-teh-o *(verb)*: Seek *Freq:* 119
**Heb#:**1245 בקש / ba-qash *(verb)*: Search out—To intently look for someone or something until the object of the search is found.

**Grk#:2222** ζωη / dzo-ay *(noun)*: Life *Freq:* 134
**Heb#:**2416 חי / hhai *(noun)*: Living—The quality that distinguishes a vital and functional being from a dead body; life. Literally the stomach. Used idiomatically of

living creatures, especially in conjunction with land, ground or field.

**Grk#:2226** ζωον / dzo-on *(noun)*: Beast *Freq:* 23
**Heb#:2416** חי / hhai *(noun)*: Living—The quality that distinguishes a vital and functional being from a dead body; life. Literally the stomach. Used idiomatically of living creatures, especially in conjunction with land, ground or field.

**Grk#:2232** ηγεμων / hayg-em-ohn *(noun)*: Governor *Freq:* 22
**Heb#:441** אלוף / a-luph *(noun)*: Chief—Accorded highest rank or office; of greatest importance, significance, or influence. The military commander of a thousand men. One who is yoked to another to lead and teach.

**Grk#:2240** ηκω / hay-ko *(verb)*: Come *Freq:* 27
**Heb#:935** בוא / bo *(verb)*: Come—To move toward something; approach; enter. This can be understood as to come or to go.

**Grk#:2243** Ηλιας / hay-lee-as *(name)*: Elijah *Freq:* 30
**Heb#:452** אליהו / ey-li-ya-hu *(name)*: Eliyahu—A personal name of Hebrew origin meaning "My God is Yahweh."

**Grk#:2246** ηλιος / hay-lee-os *(noun)*: Sun *Freq:* 32
**Heb#:8121** שמש / she-mesh *(noun)*: Sun—The luminous body around which the earth revolves and from which it receives heat and light.

**Grk#:2250** ημερα / hay-mer-ah *(noun)*: Day *Freq:* 389
**Heb#:3117** יום / yom *(noun)*: Day—The time between one dusk and the next one. Usually in the context of daylight hours but may also refer to the entire day or even a season.

**Grk#:2264** Ηρώδης / hay-ro-dace *(name)*: Herod *Freq:* 44
**Heb#:None** הורדוס / hor-dos *(name)*: Hordos—A Hebrew transliteration of a personal name of Greek origin meaning "Descendent of heroes."

**Grk#:2268** Ησαιας / hay-sah-ee-as *(name)*: Isaiah *Freq:* 21
**Heb#:3470** ישעיהו / y-sha-ya-hu *(name)*: Yeshayahu—A personal name of Hebrew origin meaning "Yahweh has saved."

**Grk#:2281** θαλασσα / thal-as-sah *(noun)*: Sea *Freq:* 92
**Heb#:3220** ים / yam *(noun)*: Sea—A large body of water. Also, the direction of the great sea (the Mediterranean), the west.

**Grk#:2288** θανατος / than-at-os *(noun)*: Death *Freq:* 119
**Heb#:4194** מות / mot *(noun)*: Death—A permanent cessation of all vital functions; the end of life.

**Grk#:2296** θαυμαζω / thou-mad-zo *(verb)*: Marvel *Freq:* 47
**Heb#:5375** נשא / na-sa *(verb)*: Lift up—To lift up a burden or load and carry it; to lift up camp and begin a journey; to forgive in the sense of removing the offense.

**Grk#:**2300 θεαομαι / theh-ah-om-ahee *(verb)*: See *Freq:* 24
 **Heb#:**7200 ראה / ra-ah *(verb)*: See—To take notice; to perceive something or someone; to see visions.

**Grk#:**2307 θελημα / thel-ay-mah *(noun)*: Will *Freq:* 64
 **Heb#:**2656 חפץ / hhey-phets *(noun)*: Delight—An object or action that one desires.
 **Heb#:**7522 רצון / ra-tson *(noun)*: Self will—Used to express determination, insistence, persistence, or willfulness. One's desire.

**Grk#:**2316 θεος / theh-os *(noun)*: God *Freq:* 1343
 **Heb#:**410 אל / el *(noun)*: Mighty one—One who holds authority over others, such as a judge, chief or god. In the sense of being yoked to one another.
 **Heb#:**430 אלוהים / e-lo-him *(noun)*: Elohiym—A plural word literally meaning "mighty ones," but often used in a singular sense to mean "the mighty one."

**Grk#:**2323 θεραπευω / ther-ap-yoo-o *(verb)*: Heal *Freq:* 44
 **Heb#:**5647 עבד / a-vad *(verb)*: Serve—To provide a service to another, as a servant or slave or to work at a profession.
 **Heb#:**7495 רפא / ra-pha *(verb)*: Heal—To restore to health or wholeness.

**Grk#:**2325 θεριζω / ther-id-zo *(verb)*: Reap *Freq:* 21
 **Heb#:**7114 קצר / qa-tsar *(verb)*: Sever—To cut short or small; to harvest in the sense of severing the crop from its stalk; to be impatient in the sense of patience being severed.

**Grk#:2334** θεωρεω / theh-o-reh-o *(verb)*: See *Freq:* 57
**Heb#:7200** ראה / ra-ah *(verb)*: See—To take notice; to perceive something or someone; to see visions.

**Grk#:2342** θηριον / thay-ree-on *(noun)*: Beast *Freq:* 46
**Heb#:2416** חי / hhai *(noun)*: Living—The quality that distinguishes a vital and functional being from a dead body; life. Literally the stomach. Used idiomatically of living creatures, especially in conjunction with land, ground or field.

**Grk#:2347** θλιψις / thlip-sis *(noun)*: Affliction *Freq:* 45
**Heb#:3906** לחץ / la-hhats *(noun)*: Squeezing—Pressure being exerted, either physically or emotionally.
**Heb#:6040** עני / a-ni *(noun)*: Affliction—The cause of persistent suffering, pain or distress.
**Heb#:6869** צרה / tsa-rah *(noun)*: Persecution—To agitate mentally or spiritually; worry; disturb.

**Grk#:2362** θρονος / thron-os *(noun)*: Seat *Freq:* 61
**Heb#:3678** כיסא / ki-sey *(noun)*: Seat—A special chair of one in eminence. Usually a throne or seat of authority.

**Grk#:2364** θυγατηρ / thoo-gat-air *(noun)*: Daughter *Freq:* 29
**Heb#:1323** בת / bat *(noun)*: Daughter—A female having the relation of a child to parent. A village that resides outside of the city walls; as "the daughter of the city."

**Grk#:2374** θυρα / thoo-rah *(noun)*: Door *Freq:* 39
**Heb#:6607** פתח / pe-tahh *(noun)*: Opening—Something that is open, as an entrance or opening of a tent, house or city.

**Grk#:**2378 θυσια / thoo-see-ah *(noun)*: Sacrifice *Freq:* 29
    **Heb#:**2077 זבח / ze-vahh *(noun)*: Sacrifice—An animal killed for an offering.
    **Heb#:**4503 מינחה / min-hhah *(noun)*: Donation—The act of making a gift or a free contribution. What is brought to another as a gift.

**Grk#:**2379 θυσιαστηριον / thoo-see-astay-ree-on *(noun)*: Altar *Freq:* 23
    **Heb#:**4196 מזבח / miz-bey-ahh *(noun)*: Altar—The place of sacrifice.

**Grk#:**2381 Θωμας / tho-mas *(name)*: Thomas *Freq:* 12
    **Heb#:**None תומא / to-ma *(name)*: Toma—A personal name of Aramaic origin meaning "Twin."

**Grk#:**2384 Ιακωβ / ee-ak-obe *(name)*: Jacob *Freq:* 27
    **Heb#:**3290 יעקוב / ya-a-qov *(name)*: Ya'aqov—A personal name of Hebrew origin meaning "He grabs the heel."

**Grk#:**2385 Ιακωβος / ee-ak-o-bos *(name)*: James *Freq:* 42
    **Heb#:**3290 יעקוב / ya-a-qov *(name)*: Ya'aqov —A personal name of Hebrew origin meaning "He grabs the heel."

**Grk#:**2390 ιαομαι / ee-ah-om-ahee *(verb)*: Heal *Freq:* 28
    **Heb#:**7495 רפא / ra-pha *(verb)*: Heal—To restore to health or wholeness.

**Grk#:**2409 ιερευς / hee-er-yooce *(noun)*: Priest *Freq:* 32
**Heb#:**3548 כּוֹהֵן / ko-heyn *(noun)*: Administrator—One who manages the affairs and activities of an organization. The administrators (often translated as "priest") of Israel are Levites who manage the Tent of Meeting, and later the Temple, as well as teach the people the teachings and directions of Yahweh, and perform other duties, such as the inspection of people and structures for disease.

**Grk#:**2411 ιερον / hee-er-on *(noun)*: Temple *Freq:* 71
**Heb#:**1964 הֵיכָל / hey-khal *(noun)*: House—The residence of a god (temple) or king (palace).

**Grk#:**2414 Ιεροσολυμα / hee-er-os-ol-oo-mah *(name)*: Jerusalem *Freq:* 59
**Heb#:**3389 ירושלם / y-ru-sha-lam *(name)*: Yerushalam— A place name of Hebrew origin meaning "Teach completeness."

**Grk#:**2419 Ιερουσαλημ / hee-er-oo-sal-ame *(name)*: Jerusalem *Freq:* 83
**Heb#:**3389 ירושלם / y-ru-sha-lam *(name)*: Yerushalam— A place name of Hebrew origin meaning "Teach completeness."

**Grk#:**2424 Ιησους / ee-ay-sooce *(name)*: Jesus *Freq:* 975
**Heb#:**3442 ישוע / y-shu-a *(name)*: Yeshua—A personal name of Aramaic origin meaning "He saves."

**Grk#:**2440 ιματιον / him-at-ee-on *(noun)*: Garment *Freq:* 61
**Heb#:**899 בגד / be-ged *(noun)*: Garment—An article of clothing for covering.

**Heb#:**8071 שימלה / sim-lah *(noun)*: Apparel—Something that clothes or adorns. As forming to the image of the body.

**Grk#:**2446 Ιορδανης / ee-or-dan-ace *(name)*: Jordan *Freq:* 15
**Heb#:**3383 ירדן / yar-den *(name)*: Yarden—A place name of Hebrew origin meaning "He descends."

**Grk#:**2449 Ιουδαια / ee-oo-dah-yah *(name)*: Judea *Freq:* 44
**Heb#:**3063 יהודה / ye-hu-dah *(name)*: Yehudah—A personal and place name of Hebrew origin meaning "Praised."

**Grk#:**2455 Ιουδας / ee-oo-das *(name)*: Judas *Freq:* 45
**Heb#:**3063 יהודה / ye-hu-dah *(name)*: Yehudah—A personal and place name of Hebrew origin meaning "Praised."

**Grk#:**2464 Ισαακ / ee-sah-ak *(name)*: Isaac *Freq:* 20
**Heb#:**3327 יצחק / yits-hhaq *(name)*: Yits'hhaq—A personal name of Hebrew origin meaning "Laughter."

**Grk#:**2474 Ισραηλ / is-rah-ale *(name)*: Israel *Freq:* 70
**Heb#:**3478 ישראל / yis-ra-eyl *(name)*: Yis'ra'el—A personal and place name of Hebrew origin meaning "He turns El."

**Grk#:**2476 ιστημι / his-tay-mee *(verb)*: Stand *Freq:* 158
**Heb#:**5324 נצב / na-tsav *(verb)*: Stand up—To be vertical in position; to stand tall and erect; to set in place.
**Heb#:**5975 עמד / a-mad *(verb)*: Stand—To rise, raise or set in a place.

**Grk#:**2478 ισχυρος / is-khoo-ros *(adj)*: Mighty *Freq:* 27
**Heb#:**2389 חזק / hha-zaq *(noun)*: Forceful—A strong grip on something to refrain or support. Driven with force. Acting with power.

**Grk#:**2491 Ιωαννης / ee-o-an-nace *(name)*: John *Freq:* 133
**Heb#:**3110 יוחנן / yo-hha-nan *(name)*: Yochanan—A personal name of Hebrew origin meaning "Yahweh has graced."

**Grk#:**2501 Ιωσηφ / ee-o-safe *(name)*: Joseph *Freq:* 35
**Heb#:**3130 יוסף / yo-seph *(name)*: Yoseph—A personal name of Hebrew origin meaning "Adding."

**Grk#:**2511 καθαριζω / kath-ar-id-zo *(verb)*: Cleanse *Freq:* 30
**Heb#:**2891 טהר / ta-har *(verb)*: Be clean—Free from dirt, pollution or immorality; unadulterated, pure. {The Greek word καθαριζω is a translation of the hiphil (causative) form of the Hebrew verb טהר meaning "make clean."}

**Grk#:**2513 καθαρος / kath-ar-os *(adj)*: Clean *Freq:* 28
**Heb#:**2889 טהור / ta-hor *(noun)*: Pure—Unmixed with any other matter. A man, animal or object that is free of impurities or is not mixed.

**Grk#:**2518 καθευδω / kath-yoo-do *(verb)*: Sleep *Freq:* 22
**Heb#:**7901 שכב / sha-khav *(verb)*: Lay down—To give up; to lie down for copulation, rest or sleep.

**Grk#:2521** καθημαι / kath-ay-mahee *(verb)*: Sit *Freq:* 89
**Heb#:3427** ישב / ya-shav *(verb)*: Settle—To stay in a dwelling place for the night or for long periods of time; to sit down.

**Grk#:2523** καθιζω / kath-id-zo *(verb)*: Sit *Freq:* 48
**Heb#:3427** ישב / ya-shav *(verb)*: Settle—To stay in a dwelling place for the night or for long periods of time; to sit down.

**Grk#:2537** καινος / kahee-nos *(adj)*: New *Freq:* 44
**Heb#:2319** חדש / hha-dash *(noun)*: New—Something that is new, renewed, restored or repaired.

**Grk#:2540** καιρος / kahee-ros *(noun)*: Time *Freq:* 87
**Heb#:4150** מועד / mo-eyd *(noun)*: Appointed—A person, place, thing or time that is fixed or officially set.
**Heb#:6256** עת / eyt *(noun)*: Appointed time—A fixed or officially set event, occasion or date.

**Grk#:2541** Καισαρ / kah-ee-sar *(name)*: Caesar *Freq:* 30
**Heb#:None** קיסר / qai-sar *(name)*: Qaisar—A Hebrew transliteration of a title of Latin origin meaning "Severed."

**Grk#:2542** Καισαρεια / kahee-sar-i-a *(name)*: Caesarea *Freq:* 17
**Heb#:None** קיסרין / qis-rin *(name)*: Qiysriyn—A Hebrew transliteration of a place name of Latin origin meaning "Severed."

**Grk#:2556** κακος / kak-os *(adj)*: Evil *Freq:* 51

  **Heb#:7451** רע / ra *(noun)*: Dysfunctional—Impaired or abnormal action other than that for which a person or thing is intended. Something that does not function within its intended purpose.

  **Heb#:7563** רשע / re-sha *(noun)*: Lost— Departed from the correct path or way, either out of ignorance or revolt.

**Grk#:2564** καλεω / kal-eh-o *(verb)*: Call *Freq:* 146

  **Heb#:7121** קרא / qa-ra *(verb)*: Call out—To raise one's voice or speak loudly and with urgency; to give a name; to meet in the sense of being called to a meeting; to have an encounter by chance; to read out loud in the sense of calling out words.

**Grk#:2570** καλος / kal-os *(adj)*: Good *Freq:* 102

  **Heb#:2896** טוב / tov *(noun)*: Functional— Fulfilling the action for which a person or thing is specially fitted or used, or for which a thing exists. A functioning within its intended purpose.

**Grk#:2573** καλως / kal-oce *(adv)*: Well *Freq:* 37

  **Heb#:2896** טוב / tov *(noun)*: Functional— Fulfilling the action for which a person or thing is specially fitted or used, or for which a thing exists. A functioning within its intended purpose.

**Grk#:2584** Καπερναουμ / cap-er-nah-oom *(name)*: Capernaum *Freq:* 16

  **Heb#:None** כפר-נחום / ke-phar na-hhum *(name)*: Kephar Nahhum—A place name of Hebrew origin meaning "Village of comfort."

**Grk#:**2588 καρδια / kar-dee-ah *(noun)*: Heart *Freq:* 160

**Heb#:**3824 לבב / ley-vav *(noun)*: Mind—Literally, the vital organ which pumps blood, but, also seen as the seat of thought; the mind.

**Heb#:**3820 לב / leyv *(noun)*: Heart—Literally, the vital organ which pumps blood, but, also seen as the seat of thought; the mind.

**Grk#:**2590 καρπος / kar-pos *(noun)*: Fruit *Freq:* 66

**Heb#:**6529 פרי / pe-ri *(noun)*: Produce—Agricultural products, especially fresh fruits and vegetables. The harvested product of a crop.

**Grk#:**2597 καταβαινω / kat-ab-ah-ee-no *(verb)*: Come down *Freq:* 81

**Heb#:**3381 ירד / ya-rad *(verb)*: Go down—To go or come lower from a higher place.

**Grk#:**2641 καταλειπω / kat-al-i-po *(verb)*: Leave *Freq:* 25

**Heb#:**3498 יתר / ya-tar *(verb)*: Leave behind—To set aside; to retain or hold over to a future time or place; to leave a remainder.

**Heb#:**5800 עזב / a-zav *(verb)*: Leave—To go away from; to neglect.

**Heb#:**7604 שאר / sha-ar *(verb)*: Remain—To continue unchanged; to stay behind.

**Grk#:**2673 καταργεω / kat-arg-eh-o *(verb)*: Abolish *Freq:* 27

**Heb#:**989 בטל / ba-tal *(verb)*: Halt—To stop an action through hindrance.

**Grk#:2716** κατεργαζομαι / kat-er-gad-zom-ahee *(verb)*: Accomplish *Freq: 24*
> **Heb#:4399** מלאכה / me-la-khah *(noun)*: Business—The principal occupation of one's life. A service.
> **Heb#:6466** פעל / pa-al *(verb)*: Make—To perform a task of physical labor.

**Grk#:2730** κατοικεω / kat-oy-keh-o *(verb)*: Dwell *Freq: 47*
> **Heb#:3427** ישב / ya-shav *(verb)*: Settle—To stay in a dwelling place for the night or for long periods of time; to sit down.

**Grk#:2744** καυχαομαι / kow-khah-om-ahee *(verb)*: Boast *Freq: 38*
> **Heb#:1984** הלל / ha-lal *(verb)*: Shine—To emit rays of light. Shine brightly. To shine or cause another to shine through one's actions or words.

**Grk#:2749** κειμαι / ki-mahee *(verb)*: Lie down *Freq: 26*
> **Heb#:3259** יעד / ya-ad *(verb)*: Appoint—To arrange, fix or set in place, to determine a set place or time to meet.

**Grk#:2753** κελευω / kel-yoo-o *(verb)*: Command *Freq: 27*
> **Heb#:6680** צוה / tsa-vah *(verb)*: Direct—To cause to turn, move, or point undeviatingly or to follow a straight course; give instructions or orders for a path to be taken.

**Grk#:2776** κεφαλη / kef-al-ay *(noun)*: Head *Freq: 76*
> **Heb#:7218** ראש / rosh *(noun)*: Head—The top of the body. A person in authority or role of leader. The top, beginning or first of something.

**Grk#:**2784 κηρυσσω / kay-roos-so *(verb)*: Preach *Freq:* 61
**Heb#:**7121 קרא / qa-ra *(verb)*: Call out—To raise one's voice or speak loudly and with urgency; to give a name; to meet in the sense of being called to a meeting; to have an encounter by chance; to read out loud in the sense of calling out words.

**Grk#:**2799 κλαιω / klah-yo *(verb)*: Weep *Freq:* 40
**Heb#:**1058 בכה / ba-khah *(verb)*: Weep—To express deep sorrow, especially by shedding tears.

**Grk#:**2836 κοιλια / koy-lee-ah *(noun)*: Womb *Freq:* 23
**Heb#:**990 בטן / be-ten *(noun)*: Womb—An organ where something is generated or grows before birth.
**Heb#:**1512 גחון / ga-hhon *(noun)*: Belly—The undersurface of an animal; the stomach and other digestive organs.

**Grk#:**2872 κοπιαω / kop-ee-ah-o *(verb)*: Labor *Freq:* 23
**Heb#:**3021 יגע / ya-ga *(verb)*: Weary—To be tired from vigorous work.

**Grk#:**2889 κοσμος / kos-mos *(noun)*: World *Freq:* 187
**Heb#:**5769 עולם / o-lam *(noun)*: Distant—A far off place as hidden beyond the horizon. A far off time as hidden from the present; the distant past or future. A place or time that cannot be perceived.

**Grk#:**2896 κραζω / krad-zo *(verb)*: Cry *Freq:* 59
**Heb#:**2199 זעק / za-aq *(verb)*: Yell out—To call out in a louder than normal voice; to declare; to cry out for help.

**Grk#:**2902 κρατεω / krat-eh-o *(verb)*: Hold *Freq:* 47
**Heb#:**270 אחז / a-hhaz *(verb)*: Take hold—To have possession or ownership of; to keep in restraint; to have or maintain in one's grasp; to grab something and keep hold of it.

**Grk#:**2917 κριμα / kree-mah *(noun)*: Judgment *Freq:* 28
**Heb#:**4941 משפט / mish-pat *(noun)*: Decision—A pronounced opinion.

**Grk#:**2919 κρινω / kree-no *(verb)*: Judge *Freq:* 114
**Heb#:**1777 דין / diyn *(verb)*: Moderate—To rule over quarrels or other conflicts.
**Heb#:**7378 ריב / riv *(verb)*: Dispute—To engage in argument; to dispute or chide another in harassment or trial.
**Heb#:**8199 שפט / sha-phat *(verb)*: Decide—To make a determination in a dispute or wrong doing.

**Grk#:**2920 κρισις / kree-sis *(noun)*: Judgment *Freq:* 48
**Heb#:**4941 משפט / mish-pat *(noun)*: Decision—A pronounced opinion.

**Grk#:**2962 κυριος / koo-ree-os *(noun)*: Lord *Freq:* 748
**Heb#:**113 אדון / a-don *(noun)*: Lord—The ruler as the foundation to the community.
**Heb#:**3068 יהוה / yi-weh *(name)*: Yihweh/Yahweh—A personal name of Hebrew origin meaning "He exists."

**Grk#:**2967 κωλυω / ko-loo-o *(verb)*: Forbid *Freq:* 23
**Heb#:**3607 כלא / ka-la *(verb)*: Restrict—To confine within bounds. Hold back or prevent someone or something.

**Grk#:2968** κωμη / ko-may *(noun)*: Village *Freq:* 28
    **Heb#:1323** בת / bat *(noun)*: Daughter—A female having the relation of a child to parent. A village that resides outside of the city walls; as "the daughter of the city."

**Grk#:2976** Λαζαρος / lad-zar-os *(name)*: Lazarus *Freq:* 15
    **Heb#:499** אלעזר / el-a-zar *(name)*: Elazar—A personal name of Hebrew origin meaning "El is helper."

**Grk#:2980** λαλεω / lal-eh-o *(verb)*: Speak *Freq:* 296
    **Heb#:559** אמר / a-mar *(verb)*: Say—To speak chains of words that form sentences.
    **Heb#:1696** דבר / da-var *(verb)*: Speak—To say a careful arrangement of words or commands.

**Grk#:2983** λαμβανω / lam-ban-o *(verb)*: Receive *Freq:* 263
    **Heb#:3947** לקח / la-qahh *(verb)*: Take—To receive what is given; to gain possession by seizing.

**Grk#:2992** λαος / lah-os *(noun)*: People *Freq:* 143
    **Heb#:1471** גוי / goy *(noun)*: Nation—An area surrounded by borders and inhabited by a people of a common ancestor or origin.
    **Heb#:5971** עם / am *(noun)*: People—A large group of men or women.

**Grk#:3000** λατρευω / lat-ryoo-o *(verb)*: Serve *Freq:* 21
    **Heb#:5647** עבד / a-vad *(verb)*: Serve—To provide a service to another, as a servant or slave or to work at a profession.

**Grk#:**3004 λεγω / leg-o *(verb)*: Say *Freq:* 1343
    **Heb#:**559 אמר / a-mar *(verb)*: Say—To speak chains of words that form sentences.
    **Heb#:**1696 דבר / da-var *(verb)*: Speak—To say a careful arrangement of words or commands.

**Grk#:**3022 λευκος / lyoo-kos *(adj)*: White *Freq:* 25
    **Heb#:**3836 לבן / la-van *(noun)*: White—Free from color.

**Grk#:**3037 λιθος / lee-thos *(noun)*: Stone *Freq:* 60
    **Heb#:**68 אבן / e-ven *(noun)*: Stone—A piece of rock, often in the context of building material.

**Grk#:**3049 λογιζομαι / log-id-zom-ahee *(verb)*: Think *Freq:* 41
    **Heb#:**2803 חשב / hha-shav *(verb)*: Think—To plan or design a course of action, item or invention.

**Grk#:**3056 λογος / log-os *(noun)*: Word *Freq:* 330
    **Heb#:**1697 דבר / da-var *(noun)*: Word—An arrangement of words, ideas or concepts to form sentences. An action in the sense of acting out an arrangement. A plague as an act.

**Grk#:**3076 λυπεω / loo-peh-o *(verb)*: Be sorrowful *Freq:* 26
    **Heb#:**2734 חרה / hha-rah *(verb)*: Flare up—To become suddenly excited or angry; to break out suddenly. Burn with a fierce anger.
    **Heb#:**7107 קצף / qa-tsaph *(verb)*: Snap—To make a sudden closing; to break suddenly with a sharp sound; to splinter a piece of wood; to lash out in anger as a splintering.

**Heb#:**6087 עצב / a-tsav *(verb)*: Distress—The state of being in great trouble, great physical or mental strain and stress. To be in pain from grief or heavy toil.

**Grk#:**3089 λυω / loo-o *(verb)*: Loose *Freq:* 43
**Heb#:**6605 פתח / pa-tahh *(verb)*: Open—To open up as opening a gate or door; to have no confining barrier.

**Grk#:**3101 μαθητης / math-ay-tes *(noun)*: Disciple *Freq:* 269
**Heb#:**8527 תלמיד / tal-mid *(noun)*: Student—One who is instructed by a teacher.

**Grk#:**3107 μακαριος / mak-ar-ee-os *(adj)*: Happy *Freq:* 50
**Heb#:**835 אשר / a-sheyr *(noun)*: Happy—A feeling of joy or satisfaction.

**Grk#:**3109 Μακεδονια / mak-ed-on-ee-ah *(name)*: Macedonia *Freq:* 24
**Heb#:**None מוקדון / muq-don *(name)*: Muqdon—A Hebrew transliteration of a place name of unknown origin meaning "Large."

**Grk#:**3129 μανθανω / man-than-o *(verb)*: Learn *Freq:* 25
**Heb#:**3925 למד / la-mad *(verb)*: Learn—To acquire knowledge or skill through instruction from one who is experienced.

**Grk#:**3136 Μαρθα / mar-thah *(name)*: Martha *Freq:* 13
**Heb#:**None מרתא / mar-ta *(name)*: Marta—A personal name of Aramaic origin meaning "Rebellious."

**Grk#:**3137 Μαρια / mar-ee-ah *(name)*: Mary *Freq:* 54
    **Heb#:**4813 מירים / mir-yam *(name)*: Miyryam—A personal name of Hebrew origin meaning "Bitter."

**Grk#:**3140 μαρτυρεω / mar-too-reh-o *(verb)*: Bear witness *Freq:* 79
    **Heb#:**5707 עד / eyd *(noun)*: Witness—Attestation of a fact or event. An object, person or group that affords evidence.
    **Heb#:**5749 עוד / ud *(verb)*: Wrap around—To enclose; to repeat or do again what has been said or done.

**Grk#:**3141 μαρτυρια / mar-too-ree-ah *(noun)*: Witness *Freq:* 37
    **Heb#:**5715 עדות / ey-dut *(noun)*: Evidence—That which proves or disproves something; something that makes plain or clear; an indication or sign.

**Grk#:**3144 μαρτυς / mar-toos *(noun)*: Witness *Freq:* 34
    **Heb#:**5707 עד / eyd *(noun)*: Witness—Attestation of a fact or event. An object, person or group that affords evidence.

**Grk#:**3162 μαχαιρα / makh-ahee-rah *(noun)*: Sword *Freq:* 29
    **Heb#:**2719 חרב / hhe-rev *(noun)*: Sword—A weapon with a long blade for cutting or thrusting.

**Grk#:**3187 μειζων / mide-zone *(adj)*: Greater *Freq:* 45
    **Heb#:**1419 גדול / ga-dol *(noun)*: Great—Something with increased size, power or authority.
    **Heb#:**7227 רב / rav *(noun)*: Abundant—Great plenty or supply of numbers (many) or strength (great). One who is

abundant in authority such as a master or teacher. Also, an archer as one abundant with arrows.

**Grk#:**3196 μελος / mel-os *(noun)*: Member *Freq:* 34
    **Heb#:**5409 נתח / ney-tahh *(noun)*: Piece—A part of the original. What has been cut from the whole.

**Grk#:**3306 μενω / men-o *(verb)*: Abide *Freq:* 120
    **Heb#:**3427 ישב / ya-shav *(verb)*: Settle—To stay in a dwelling place for the night or for long periods of time; to sit down.
    **Heb#:**3885 לון / lun *(verb)*: Lodge—To remain or stay through the night.

**Grk#:**3313 μερος / mer-os *(noun)*: Part *Freq:* 43
    **Heb#:**1290 ברך / be-rekh *(noun)*: Knee—The joint between the femur and tibia of the leg.
    **Heb#:**3409 ירך / ya-rey-akh *(noun)*: Midsection—The lower abdomen and back.

**Grk#:**3319 μεσος / mes-os *(adj)*: Among *Freq:* 61
    **Heb#:**7130 קרב / qe-rev *(noun)*: Within—In the sense of being close or in the interior of. An approaching.
    **Heb#:**8432 תוך / ta-vek *(noun)*: Midst—The center or middle of the whole.

**Grk#:**3340 μετανοεω / met-an-o-eh-o *(verb)*: Repent *Freq:* 34
    **Heb#:**5162 נחם / na-hham *(verb)*: Comfort—Consolation in time of trouble or worry; to give solace in time of difficulty or sorrow. {The Greek word μετανοεω is a translation of the hiphil (causative) form of the Hebrew

verb נחם meaning "repent" through the idea of "being comforted."}

**Grk#:**3341 μετανοια / met-an-oy-ah *(noun)*: Repentance *Freq:* 24

    **Heb#:**5164 נוחם / no-hham *(noun)*: Sorrow—An emotion during time of difficulty.
    **Heb#:**7725 שוב / shuv *(verb)*: Turn back—To return to a previous place or state.

**Grk#:**3384 μητηρ / may-tare *(noun)*: Mother *Freq:* 85

    **Heb#:**517 אם / eym *(noun)*: Mother—A female parent. Maternal tenderness or affection. One who fulfills the role of a mother.

**Grk#:**3391 μια / mee-ah *(adj)*: One *Freq:* 79

    **Heb#:**259 אחד / e-hhad *(noun)*: Unit—A unit within the whole, a unified group. A single quantity.

**Grk#:**3398 μικρος / mik-ros *(adj)*: Little *Freq:* 30

    **Heb#:**4592 מעט / me-at *(noun)*: Small amount—Something that is few or small in size or amount.
    **Heb#:**6996 קטן / qa-tan *(noun)*: Small—Someone or something that is not very large in size, importance, age or significance.

**Grk#:**3404 μισεω / mis-eh-o *(verb)*: Hate *Freq:* 42

    **Heb#:**8130 שנא / sa-na *(verb)*: Hate—Intense hostility and aversion, usually deriving from fear, anger, or sense of injury; extreme dislike or antipathy.

**Grk#:**3408 μισθος / mis-thos *(noun)*: Reward *Freq:* 29
**Heb#:**7939 שכר / se-kher *(noun)*: Wage—The reward or price paid for one's labor.

**Grk#:**3415 μιμνησκομαι / mim-ney-sko-mai *(verb)*: Remember *Freq:* 21
**Heb#:**2142 זכר / za-khar *(verb)*: Remember—To act or speak on behalf of another. To reenact a past event as a memorial.

**Grk#:**3419 μνημειον / mnay-mi-on *(noun)*: Sepulchre *Freq:* 42
**Heb#:**6913 קבר / qe-ver *(noun)*: Grave—An excavation for the burial of a body.

**Grk#:**3421 μνημονευω / mnay-mon-yoo-o *(verb)*: Remember *Freq:* 21
**Heb#:**2142 זכר / za-khar *(verb)*: Remember—To act or speak on behalf of another. To reenact a past event as a memorial.

**Grk#:**3466 μυστηριον / moos-tay-ree-on *(noun)*: Mystery *Freq:* 27
**Heb#:**7328 רז / raz *(noun)*: Secret—Something that is hidden.

**Grk#:**3475 Μωυσης / mo-oo-sace *(name)*: Moses *Freq:* 80
**Heb#:**4872 מושה / mo-sheh *(name)*: Mosheh—A personal name of Hebrew origin meaning "Drawn out."

**Grk#:**3478 Ναζαρεθ / nad-zar-eth *(name)*: Nazareth *Freq:* 12
**Heb#:**None נצרת / ne-tsa-ret *(name)*: Netsaret—A place name of Hebrew origin meaning "Guarding."

**Grk#:**3480 Ναζωραιος / nad-zo-rah-yos *(name)*: Nazarene *Freq:* 15
    **Heb#:**None נצרת / ne-tsa-ret *(name)*: Netsaret—A place name of Hebrew origin meaning "Guarding."

**Grk#:**3485 ναος / nah-os *(noun)*: Temple *Freq:* 46
    **Heb#:**1964 היכל / hey-khal *(noun)*: Palace—The residence of a god (temple) or king (palace).

**Grk#:**3498 νεκρος / nek-ros *(adj)*: Dead *Freq:* 132
    **Heb#:**4191 מות / mut *(verb)*: Die—To pass from physical life; to pass out of existence; to come to an end through death.

**Grk#:**3501 νεος / neh-os *(adj)*: Young *Freq:* 24
    **Heb#:**2319 חדש / hha-dash *(noun)*: New—Something that is new, renewed, restored or repaired.
    **Heb#:**5288 נער / na-ar *(noun)*: Young man—A male that has moved from youth to young adulthood.
    **Heb#:**6810 צעיר / tsa-ir *(noun)*: Little one—Small in size or extent. Something or someone that is smaller, younger or less significant.
    **Heb#:**6996 קטן / qa-tan *(noun)*: Small—Someone or something that is not very large in size, importance, age or significance.

**Grk#:**3507 νεφελη / nef-el-ay *(noun)*: Cloud *Freq:* 26
    **Heb#:**6051 ענן / a-nan *(noun)*: Cloud—A visible mass of particles of water or ice in the form of fog, mist, or haze suspended usually at a considerable height in the air.

**Grk#:**3551 νομος / nom-os *(noun)*: Law *Freq:* 197
**Heb#:**8451 תורה / to-rah *(noun)*: Teaching—Acquired knowledge or skills that mark the direction one is to take in life. A straight direction. Knowledge passed from one person to another.

**Grk#:**3563 νους / nooce *(noun)*: Mind *Freq:* 24
**Heb#:**3820 לב / leyv *(noun)*: Heart—Literally, the vital organ which pumps blood, but, also seen as the seat of thought; the mind.

**Grk#:**3571 νυξ / noox *(noun)*: Night *Freq:* 65
**Heb#:**3915 ליל / la-yil *(noun)*: Night—The time from dusk to dawn. The hours associated with darkness and sleep.

**Grk#:**3598 οδος / hod-os *(noun)*: Way *Freq:* 102
**Heb#:**1870 דרך / de-rek *(noun)*: Road—A route or path traveled or walked. The path or manner of life.

**Grk#:**3614 οικια / oy-kee-ah *(noun)*: House *Freq:* 95
**Heb#:**1004 בית / beyt *(noun)*: House—The structure or the family, as a household that resides within the house. A housing. Within.

**Grk#:**3618 οικοδομεω / oy-kod-om-eh-o *(verb)*: Build *Freq:* 39
**Heb#:**1129 בנה / ba-nah *(verb)*: Build—To construct a building with wood, stone or other material or a family with sons.

**Grk#:**3624 οικος / oy-kos *(noun)*: House *Freq:* 114
**Heb#:**1004 בית / beyt *(noun)*: House—The structure or the family, as a household that resides within the house. A housing. Within.

**Grk#:**3631 οινος / oy-nos *(noun)*: Wine *Freq:* 33
**Heb#:**3196 יין / ya-yin *(noun)*: Wine—Fermented juice of fresh grapes.

**Grk#:**3641 ολιγος / ol-ee-gos *(adj)*: Few *Freq:* 43
**Heb#:**4592 מעט / me-at *(noun)*: Small amount—Something that is few or small in size or amount.

**Grk#:**3650 ολος / ho-los *(adj)*: All *Freq:* 112
**Heb#:**3605 כול / kol *(noun)*: All—The whole of a group.

**Grk#:**3660 ομνυω / om-noo-o *(verb)*: Swear *Freq:* 27
**Heb#:**7650 שבע / sha-va *(verb)*: Swear—To completely submit to a promise or oath with words and spoken seven times.

**Grk#:**3670 ομολογεω / hom-ol-og-eh-o *(verb)*: Confess *Freq:* 24
**Heb#:**3034 ידה / ya-dah *(verb)*: Throw the hand—To stretch out the hand to grab; to show praise or confession. {The Greek word ομολογεω is a translation of the hiphil (causative) form of the Hebrew verb ידה meaning "to confess" in the sense of causing one to throw the hand out in regret.}

**Grk#:**3686 ονομα / on-om-ah *(noun)*: Name *Freq:* 230
**Heb#:**8034 שם / sheym *(noun)*: Title—A word given to an individual or place denoting its character. The character of an individual or place.

**Grk#:**3694 οπισω / op-is-o *(adv)*: After *Freq:* 36
**Heb#:**310 אחרי / a-hhar-i *(adj)*: After—A time to come beyond another event.

**Grk#:**3700 οπτανομαι / op-tan-om-ahee *(verb)*: See/Appear *Freq:* 58
**Heb#:**7200 ראה / ra-ah *(verb)*: See—To take notice; to perceive something or someone; to see visions. {The Greek word οπτανομαι may also be the translation of the niphil (passive) form of the Hebrew verb ראה meaning "be seen," or "appear."}

**Grk#:**3708 οραω / hor-ah-o *(verb)*: See *Freq:* 59
**Heb#:**7200 ראה / ra-ah *(verb)*: See—To take notice; to perceive something or someone; to see visions.

**Grk#:**3709 οργη / or-gay *(noun)*: Wrath *Freq:* 36
**Heb#:**639 אף / aph *(noun)*: Nose—The organ bearing the nostrils on the anterior of the face. The nostrils when used in the plural form. Also meaning anger from the flaring of the nostrils and the redness of the nose when angry.

**Grk#:**3735 ορος / or-os *(noun)*: Mountain *Freq:* 65
**Heb#:**2022 הר / har *(noun)*: Hill—An elevation of land such as a hill or mountain.

**Grk#:**3772 ουρανος / oo-ran-os *(noun)*: Heaven *Freq:* 284
   **Heb#:**8064 שמים / sha-ma-yim *(noun)*: Sky—The upper atmosphere that constitutes an apparent great vault or arch over the earth. Place of the winds.

**Grk#:**3788 οφθαλμος / of-thal-mos *(noun)*: Eye *Freq:* 102
   **Heb#:**5869 עין / a-yin *(noun)*: Eye—The organ of sight or vision that tears when a person weeps. Also a spring that weeps water out of the ground.

**Grk#:**3793 οχλος / okhlos *(noun)*: Crowd *Freq:* 175
   **Heb#:**5971 עם / am *(noun)*: People—A large group of men or women.

**Grk#:**3813 παιδιον / pahee-dee-on *(noun)*: Child *Freq:* 51
   **Heb#:**3206 ילד / ye-led *(noun)*: Boy—A male child from birth to puberty.
   **Heb#:**5288 נער / na-ar *(noun)*: Young man—A male that has moved from youth to young adulthood.

**Grk#:**3816 παις / paheece *(noun)*: Servant *Freq:* 24
   **Heb#:**5650 עבד / e-ved *(noun)*: Servant—One who provides a service to another, as a slave, bondservant or hired hand.

**Grk#:**3850 παραβολη / par-ab-ol-ay *(noun)*: Parable *Freq:* 50
   **Heb#:**4912 משל / ma-shal *(noun)*: Proverb—An illustration of similitude. Often a parable or proverb as a story of comparisons.

**Grk#:3853** παραγγελλω / par-ang-gel-lo *(verb)*: Command
*Freq:* 31
> **Heb#:6680** צוה / tsa-vah *(verb)*: Direct—To cause to turn, move, or point undeviatingly or to follow a straight course; give instructions or orders for a path to be taken.

**Grk#:3854** παραγινομαι / par-ag-in-om-ahee *(verb)*: Come
*Freq:* 37
> **Heb#:935** בוא / bo *(verb)*: Come—To move toward something; approach; enter. This can be understood as to come or to go.

**Grk#:3860** παραδιδωμι / par-ad-id-o-mee *(verb)*: Deliver
*Freq:* 121
> **Heb#:5414** נתן / na-tan *(verb)*: Give—To make a present; to present a gift; to grant, allow or bestow by formal action.

**Grk#:3870** παρακαλεω / par-ak-al-eh-o *(verb)*: Beseech
*Freq:* 109
> **Heb#:5162** נחם / na-hham *(verb)*: Comfort—Consolation in time of trouble or worry; to give solace in time of difficulty or sorrow.

**Grk#:3874** παρακλησις / par-ak-lay-sis *(noun)*: Consolation
*Freq:* 29
> **Heb#:5150** ניחום / ni-hhum *(noun)*: Comfort—Consolation in time of trouble or worry
> **Heb#:8575** תנחום / tan-hhum *(noun)*: Comfort—Consolation in time of trouble or worry

**Grk#:**3880 παραλαμβανω / par-al-am-ban-o *(verb)*: Take *Freq:* 50
> **Heb#:**3947 לקח / la-qahh *(verb)*: Take—To receive what is given; to gain possession by seizing.

**Grk#:**3900 παραπτωμα / par-ap-to-mah *(noun)*: Trespass *Freq:* 23
> **Heb#:**5766 עול / ul *(noun)*: Wicked—A violation of right or duty
> **Heb#:**6588 פשע / pe-sha *(noun)*: Transgression—The exceeding of due bounds or limits.

**Grk#:**3928 παρερχομαι / par-er-khom-ahee *(verb)*: Pass away *Freq:* 31
> **Heb#:**5674 עבר / a-var *(verb)*: Cross over—To pass from one side to the other; to go across a river or through a land; to transgress in the sense of crossing over.

**Grk#:**3936 παριστημι / par-is-tay-mee *(verb)*: Stand by *Freq:* 42
> **Heb#:**5975 עמד / a-mad *(verb)*: Stand—To rise, raise or set in a place.

**Grk#:**3952 παρουσια / par-oo-see-ah *(noun)*: Coming *Freq:* 24
> **Heb#:**935 בוא / bo *(verb)*: Come—To move toward something; approach; enter. This can be understood as to come or to go.

**Grk#:**3957 πασχα / pas-khah *(noun)*: Passover *Freq:* 29
> **Heb#:**6453 פסח / pe-sahh *(noun)*: Pesahh—The day of deliverance from Egypt. Also the feast remembering this day and the lamb that is sacrificed for this feast.

**Grk#:**3958 πασχω / pas-kho *(verb)*: Suffer *Freq:* 42
**Heb#:**6031 עָנָה / a-nah *(verb)*: Afflict—To oppress severely so as to cause persistent suffering or anguish in the sense of making dark.

**Grk#:**3962 πατηρ / pat-ayr *(noun)*: Father *Freq:* 419
**Heb#:**1 אָב / av *(noun)*: Father—A man who has begotten a child. The provider and support to the household. The ancestor of a family line. The patron of a profession or art.

**Grk#:**3972 Παυλος / pow-los *(name)*: Paul *Freq:* 164
**Heb#:**None פולוס / po-los *(name)*: Polos—A Hebrew transliteration of a personal name of Latin origin meaning "Small."

**Grk#:**3982 πειθω / pi-tho *(verb)*: Persuade *Freq:* 55
**Heb#:**6601 פתה / pa-tah *(verb)*: Spread wide—To lay out in a large area. {The Greek word πειθω is the translation of the piel (intensive) form of the Hebrew word פתה meaning "persuade."}

**Grk#:**3983 πειναω / pi-nah-o *(verb)*: Hunger *Freq:* 23
**Heb#:**7458 רָעָב / ra-eyv *(noun)*: Hunger—A craving or urgent need for food.

**Grk#:**3985 πειραζω / pi-rad-zo *(verb)*: Tempt *Freq:* 39
**Heb#:**5254 נסה / na-sah *(verb)*: Test—A critical examination, observation, or evaluation; trial.

**Grk#:**3986 πειρασμος / pi-ras-mos *(noun)*: Temptation *Freq:* 21
**Heb#:**4531 מסה / ma-sah *(noun)*: Trial—The act of trying, testing, or putting to the proof.

**Grk#:**3992 πεμπω / pem-po *(verb)*: Send *Freq:* 81
**Heb#:**7971 שלח / sha-lahh *(verb)*: Send—To cause to go; to direct, order, or request to go.

**Grk#:**4002 πεντε / pen-teh *(noun)*: Five *Freq:* 38
**Heb#:**2568 חמש / hha-meysh *(noun)*: Five—A cardinal number.

**Grk#:**4008 περαν / per-an *(adv)*: Beyond *Freq:* 23
**Heb#:**5676 עבר / ey-ver *(noun)*: Other side—As being across from this side.

**Grk#:**4016 περιβαλλω / per-ee-bal-lo *(verb)*: Clothe *Freq:* 24
**Heb#:**3680 כסה / ka-sah *(verb)*: Cover over—To prevent disclosure or recognition of; to place out of sight; to completely cover over or hide.
**Heb#:**3847 לבש / la-vash *(verb)*: Wear—To cover with cloth or clothing; to provide with clothing; put on clothing. {The Greek word περιβαλλω is a translation of the hiphil (causative) form of the Hebrew verb לבש meaning "to make wear," or "clothe."}

**Grk#:**4043 περιπατεω / per-ee-pat-eh-o *(verb)*: Walk *Freq:* 96
**Heb#:**1980 הלך / ha-lakh *(verb)*: Walk—To move along on foot; walk a journey; to go. Also, customs as a lifestyle that is walked or lived.

**Grk#:**4052 περισσευω / per-is-syoo-o *(verb)*: Abound *Freq:* 39
**Heb#:**4195 מותר / mo-tar *(noun)*: Profit—An abundance of wealth or respect.

**Grk#:**4061 περιτομη / per-it-om-ay *(noun)*: Circumcision *Freq:* 36
**Heb#:**4139 מולה / mu-lah *(noun)*: Circumcision—The removal of the front part of the male sexual organ.

**Grk#:**4074 Πετρος / pet-ros *(name)*: Peter *Freq:* 162
**Heb#:**None פטרוס / pet-ros *(name)*: Petros—A Hebrew transliteration of a personal name of Greek origin meaning "Stone."

**Grk#:**4091 Πιλατος / pil-at-os *(name)*: Pilate *Freq:* 55
**Heb#:**None פילטוס / pi-la-tos *(name)*: Piylatos—A Hebrew transliteration of a personal name of Latin origin meaning "Armed with a spear."

**Grk#:**4095 πινω / pee-no *(verb)*: Drink *Freq:* 75
**Heb#:**8248 שקה / sha-qah *(verb)*: Drink—To swallow liquid, whether of man or of the land.

**Grk#:**4098 πιπτω / pip-to *(verb)*: Fall *Freq:* 90
**Heb#:**5307 נפל / na-phal *(verb)*: Fall—To leave an erect position suddenly and involuntarily; to descend freely by the force of gravity.

**Grk#:**4100 πιστευω / pist-yoo-o *(verb)*: Believe *Freq:* 248
**Heb#:**539 אמן / a-man *(verb)*: Secure—Solidly fixed in place; to stand firm in the sense of a support. Not subject to change or revision. {The Greek word πιστευω is a

translation of the hiphil (causative) form of the Hebrew verb אמן meaning "to support."}

**Grk#:4102** πιστις / pis-tis *(noun)*: Faith *Freq:* 244
**Heb#:530** אמונה / e-mu-nah *(noun)*: Firmness—Securely fixed in place.

**Grk#:4103** πιστος / pis-tos *(adj)*: Faithful *Freq:* 67
**Heb#:539** אמן / a-man *(verb)*: Secure—Solidly fixed in place; to stand firm in the sense of a support. Not subject to change or revision. {The Greek word πιστος is a translation of the participle form of the Hebrew verb אמן meaning "one who is secure."}

**Grk#:4105** πλαναω / plan-ah-o *(verb)*: Deceive *Freq:* 39
**Heb#:8582** תעה / ta-ah *(verb)*: Wander— To go astray due to deception or an outside influence. To stagger, as from being intoxicated.

**Grk#:4127** πληγη / play-gay *(noun)*: Plague *Freq:* 21
**Heb#:4347** מכה / ma-kah *(noun)*: Crushed—Pressed or squeezed with a force that destroys or deforms. Also a plague.
**Heb#:5061** נגע / ne-ga *(noun)*: Plague—An epidemic disease causing high mortality. An epidemic or other sore or illness as a touch from God.

**Grk#:4128** πληθος / play-thos *(noun)*: Multitude *Freq:* 32
**Heb#:7227** רב / rav *(noun)*: Abundant—Great plenty or supply of numbers (many) or strength (great). One who is abundant in authority such as a master or teacher. Also, an archer as one abundant with arrows.

**Heb#:**7230 רוב / rov *(noun)*: Abundance—An ample quantity of number (many) or plentiful supply of strength (great).

**Grk#:**4130 πιμπλημι / pim-play-mee *(verb)*: Fill *Freq:* 24
**Heb#:**4390 מלא / ma-la *(verb)*: Fill—To occupy to the full capacity.

**Grk#:**4137 πληροω / play-ro-o *(verb)*: Fulfil *Freq:* 90
**Heb#:**4390 מלא / ma-la *(verb)*: Fill—To occupy to the full capacity. {The Greek word πληροω is the piel (intensive) form of the Hebrew verb מלא meaning "fulfill."}
**Heb#:**7999 שלם / sha-lam *(verb)*: Make restitution—To restore or make right through action, payment or restoration to a rightful owner.

**Grk#:**4143 πλοιον / ploy-on *(noun)*: Ship *Freq:* 67
**Heb#:**591 אניה / a-ni-yah *(noun)*: Ship—A large sea-going vessel. As searching through the sea for a distant shore.

**Grk#:**4145 πλουσιος / ploo-see-os *(adj)*: Rich *Freq:* 28
**Heb#:**3515 כבד / ka-ved *(noun)*: Heavy—Having great weight. Something that is weighty. May also be grief or sadness in the sense of heaviness. Also, the liver as the heaviest of the organs.
**Heb#:**6223 עשיר / a-shir *(noun)*: Rich—Having wealth or great possessions; abundantly supplied with resources, means, or funds.

**Grk#:**4149 πλουτος / ploo-tos *(noun)*: Riches *Freq:* 22
**Heb#:**6239 עושר / o-sher *(noun)*: Riches—Wealth. The possessions that make one wealthy.

# New Testament Greek to Hebrew Dictionary

**Grk#:**4151 πνευμα / pnyoo-mah *(noun)*: Spirit/Breath *Freq:* 385
 **Heb#:**5397 נשמה / ne-shey-mah *(noun)*: Breath—Air inhaled or exhaled. The breath of man or god. The essence of life.
 **Heb#:**7307 רוח / ru-ahh *(noun)*: Wind—A natural movement of air; breath. The breath of man, animal or God. The character. A space in between.

**Grk#:**4152 πνευματικος / pnyoo-mat-ik-os *(adj)*: Spiritual *Freq:* 26
 **Heb#:**7307 רוח / ru-ahh *(noun)*: Wind—A natural movement of air; breath. The breath of man, animal or God. The character. A space in between.

**Grk#:**4160 ποιεω / poy-eh-o *(verb)*: Do *Freq:* 579
 **Heb#:**6213 עשה / a-sah *(verb)*: Do—To bring to pass; to bring about; to act or make.

**Grk#:**4172 πολις / pol-is *(noun)*: City *Freq:* 164
 **Heb#:**5892 עיר / ir *(noun)*: City—A large populace of people; a town or village.

**Grk#:**4190 πονηρος / pon-ay-ros *(adj)*: Evil *Freq:* 76
 **Heb#:**7451 רע / ra *(noun)*: Dysfunctional—Impaired or abnormal action other than that for which a person or thing is intended. Something that does not function within its intended purpose.
 **Heb#:**7563 רשע / re-sha *(noun)*: Lost— Departed from the correct path or way, either out of ignorance or revolt.

**Grk#:4198** πορευομαι / por-yoo-om-ahee *(verb)*: Go *Freq:* 154
**Heb#:1980** הלך / ha-lakh *(verb)*: Walk—To move along on foot; walk a journey; to go. Also, customs as a lifestyle that is walked or lived.

**Grk#:4202** πορνεια / por-ni-ah *(noun)*: Fornication *Freq:* 26
**Heb#:2181** זנה / za-nah *(verb)*: Be a whore—A woman who practices promiscuous sexual behavior, especially for hire.

**Grk#:4221** ποτηριον / pot-ay-ree-on *(noun)*: Cup *Freq:* 33
**Heb#:3563** כוס / kos *(noun)*: Cup—A vessel for holding liquids, usually for drinking.

**Grk#:4228** πους / pooce *(noun)*: Foot *Freq:* 93
**Heb#:7272** רגל / re-gel *(noun)*: Foot—The terminal part of the leg upon which the human, animal or object stands. Also euphemistically for the leg.

**Grk#:4238** πρασσω / pras-so *(verb)*: Do *Freq:* 38
**Heb#:6213** עשה / a-sah *(verb)*: Do—To bring to pass; to bring about; to act or make.
**Heb#:6466** פעל / pa-al *(verb)*: Make—To perform a task of physical labor.

**Grk#:4245** πρεσβυτερος / pres-boo-ter-os *(adj)*: Elder *Freq:* 67
**Heb#:2205** זקן / za-qeyn *(noun)*: Beard—The hair that grows on a man's face. A long beard as a sign of old age and wisdom. An elder as a bearded one.

**Grk#:**4263 προβατον / prob-at-on *(noun)*: Sheep *Freq:* 41
**Heb#:**3532 כשב / ke-sev *(noun)*: Sheep—A mammal related to the goat domesticated for its flesh and wool.
**Heb#:**7716 שה / seh *(noun)*: Ram—A member of a flock of sheep or goats.

**Grk#:**4334 προσερχομαι / pros-er-khom-ahee *(verb)*: Come *Freq:* 86
**Heb#:**5066 נגש / na-gash *(verb)*: Draw near—To bring close to another.

**Grk#:**4335 προσευχη / pros-yoo-khay *(noun)*: Prayer *Freq:* 37
**Heb#:**8605 תפילה / te-phi-lah *(noun)*: Pleading—To earnestly appeal to another for or against an action.

**Grk#:**4336 προσευχομαι / pros-yoo-khom-ahee *(verb)*: Pray *Freq:* 87
**Heb#:**6419 פלל / pa-lal *(verb)*: Plead—To entreat or appeal earnestly; to fall to the ground to plead a cause to one in authority; prevent a judgment.

**Grk#:**4337 προσεχω / pros-ekh-o *(verb)*: Beware *Freq:* 24
**Heb#:**8104 שמר / sha-mar *(verb)*: Safeguard—The act or the duty of protecting or defending; to watch over or guard in the sense of preserving or protecting.

**Grk#:**4341 προσκαλεομαι / pros-kal-eh-om-ahee *(verb)*: Call unto *Freq:* 30
**Heb#:**7121 קרא / qa-ra *(verb)*: Call out—To raise one's voice or speak loudly and with urgency; to give a name; to meet in the sense of being called to a meeting; to have

an encounter by chance; to read out loud in the sense of calling out words.

**Grk#:**4352 προσκυνεω / pros-koo-neh-o *(verb)*: Worship *Freq:* 60

> **Heb#:**7812 שחה / sha-hhah *(verb)*: Bend down—To pay homage to another one by bowing low or getting on the knees with the face to the ground.

**Grk#:**4374 προσφερω / pros-fer-o *(verb)*: Offer *Freq:* 48

> **Heb#:**7126 קרב / qa-rav *(verb)*: Come near—To come close by or near to.

**Grk#:**4383 προσωπον / pros-o-pon *(noun)*: Face *Freq:* 78

> **Heb#:**6440 פנים / pa-niym *(noun)*: Face—The anterior part of the human head; outward appearance. One present, in the sense of being in the face of another.

**Grk#:**4395 προφητευω / prof-ate-yoo-o *(verb)*: Prophesy *Freq:* 28

> **Heb#:**5012 נבא / na-va *(verb)*: Prophesy—To utter the words or instructions of Elohiym received through a vision or dream.

**Grk#:**4396 προφητης / prof-ay-tace *(noun)*: Prophet *Freq:* 149

> **Heb#:**5030 נביא / na-vi *(noun)*: Prophet—One who utters the words or instructions of Elohiym that are received through a vision or dream.

**Grk#:**4412 πρωτον / pro-ton *(adv)*: First *Freq:* 60

> **Heb#:**7223 ריאשון / ri-shon *(noun)*: First—The head of a time or position.

**Grk#:**4413 πρωτος / pro-tos *(adj)*: Chief *Freq:* 105
    **Heb#:**7223 ריאשון / ri-shon *(noun)*: First—The head of a time or position.
    **Heb#:**7225 ראשית / rey-shit *(noun)*: Summit—The head, top or beginning of a place, such as a river or mountain, or a time, such as an event. The point at which something starts; origin, source.

**Grk#:**4434 πτωχος / pto-ksos *(adj)*: Poor *Freq:* 34
    **Heb#:**34 אביון / ev-yon *(noun)*: Needy—In a condition of need or want.
    **Heb#:**1800 דל / dal *(noun)*: Weak—One who dangles the head in poverty or hunger.
    **Heb#:**6041 עני / a-ni *(noun)*: Affliction—The cause of persistent suffering, pain or distress.

**Grk#:**4442 πυρ / poor *(noun)*: Fire *Freq:* 74
    **Heb#:**784 אש / eysh *(noun)*: Fire—The phenomenon of combustion manifested by heat, light and flame.

**Grk#:**4453 πωλεω / po-leh-o *(verb)*: Sell *Freq:* 22
    **Heb#:**4376 מכר / ma-khar *(verb)*: Sell—To give up property to another for money or another valuable compensation.
    **Heb#:**7666 שבל / sha-val *(verb)*: Exchange—The act of giving or taking one thing in return for another. To buy or sell produce, usually grain. To barter.

**Grk#:**4483 ρεω / hreh-o *(verb)*: Speak *Freq:* 26
    **Heb#:**559 אמר / a-mar *(verb)*: Say—To speak chains of words that form sentences.

**Heb#:**1696 דבר / da-var *(verb)*: Speak—To say a careful arrangement of words or commands.

**Grk#:**4487 ρημα / hray-mah *(noun)*: Word *Freq:* 70
**Heb#:**1697 דבר / da-var *(noun)*: Word—An arrangement of words, ideas or concepts to form sentences. An action in the sense of acting out an arrangement. A plague as an act.

**Grk#:**4516 Ρωμη / hro-may *(name)*: Rome *Freq:* 14
**Heb#:**None רומא / ro-ma *(name)*: Roma—A place name of Latin origin meaning "Hard."

**Grk#:**4521 σαββατον / sab-bat-on *(noun)*: Sabbath day *Freq:* 68
**Heb#:**7676 שבת / sha-bat *(noun)*: Ceasing—A stopping of work or activity; An activity curtailed before completion. The seventh day of the week (often translated as Sabbath) when all business ceases for rest and celebration.

**Grk#:**4561 σαρξ / sarx *(noun)*: Flesh *Freq:* 151
**Heb#:**1320 בשר / ba-sar *(noun)*: Flesh—The soft parts of a human or animal, composed primarily of skeletal muscle. Skin and muscle or the whole of the person. Meat as food.

**Grk#:**4567 Σατανας / sat-an-as *(name)*: Satan *Freq:* 36
**Heb#:**7854 סטן / sa-tan *(name)*: Satan—A Hebrew noun used in Greek as a personal name.

**Grk#:**4569 Σαυλος / sow-los *(name)*: Saul *Freq:* 17
   **Heb#:**7586 שאול / sha-ul *(name)*: Sha'ul—A personal
   name of Hebrew origin meaning "Request."

**Grk#:**4592 σημειον / say-mi-on *(noun)*: Sign *Freq:* 77
   **Heb#:**226 אות / ot *(noun)*: Sign—The motion, gesture, or
   mark representing an agreement between two parties. A
   wondrous or miraculous sign.
   **Heb#:**8420 תו / tav *(noun)*: Mark—A sign or post used for
   identification.

**Grk#:**4594 σημερον / say-mer-on *(adv)*: This day *Freq:* 41
   **Heb#:**3117 יום / yom *(noun)*: Day—The time between
   one dusk and the next one. Usually in the context of
   daylight hours but may also refer to the entire day or
   even a season. {The Greek word σημερον is a translation
   of the Hebrew noun יום when it is preceded by the prefix
   ה, meaning "the" - "the day" or "today."}

**Grk#:**4613 Σιμων / see-mone *(name)*: Simon *Freq:* 75
   **Heb#:**8095 שימעון / shi-mon *(name)*: Shimon—A
   personal name of Hebrew origin meaning "Hearer."

**Grk#:**4632 σκευος / skyoo-os *(noun)*: Vessel *Freq:* 23
   **Heb#:**3627 כלי / ke-li *(noun)*: Item—A utensil or
   implement usually for carrying or storing various
   materials.

**Grk#:**4655 σκοτος / skot-os *(noun)*: Darkness *Freq:* 32
   **Heb#:**2822 חושך / hho-shekh *(noun)*: Darkness—The
   state of being dark. As the darkness of a moonless night.

**Grk#:**4672 Σολομων / sol-om-one *(name)*: Solomon *Freq:* 12
  **Heb#:**8010 שלמה / shlo-mo *(name)*: Shlomo—A personal name of Hebrew origin meaning "Completeness."

**Grk#:**4678 σοφια / sof-ee-ah *(noun)*: Wisdom *Freq:* 51
  **Heb#:**2451 חכמה / hhakh-mah *(noun)*: Skill—The ability to decide or discern between good and bad, right and wrong.

**Grk#:**4680 σοφος / sof-os *(adj)*: Wise *Freq:* 22
  **Heb#:**2450 חכם / hha-kham *(noun)*: Skilled one—A person characterized by a deep understanding of a craft.

**Grk#:**4687 σπειρω / spi-ro *(verb)*: Sow *Freq:* 54
  **Heb#:**2232 זרע / za-ra *(verb)*: Sow—To spread seeds on the ground; to plant a crop.

**Grk#:**4690 σπερμα / sper-mah *(noun)*: Seed *Freq:* 44
  **Heb#:**2233 זרע / ze-ra *(noun)*: Seed—The grains or ripened ovules of plants used for sowing. Scattered in the field to produce a crop. The singular word can be used for one or more. Also, the descendants of an individual, either male or female.

**Grk#:**4716 σταυρος / stow-ros *(noun)*: Cross/Stake *Freq:* 28
  **Heb#:**6086 עץ / eyts *(noun)*: Tree—A woody perennial plant with a supporting stem or trunk and multiple branches. {There is no Biblical Hebrew word equivalent to the Greek word σταυρος, but in Modern Hebrew translations of the New Testament the word עץ is used.}
  **Heb#:**None זקיפה / ze-qee-phah *(noun)*: Pole—An upright stake. {There is no Biblical Hebrew word

equivalent to the Greek word σταυρος, but in the Peshitta[15] the word זקיפה is used, which is derived from the verb זקף (zaqaph, Strong's Hebrew #2210) meaning "to raise up."}

**Grk#:**4717 σταυροω / stow-ro-o *(verb)*: Crucify *Freq:* 46
   **Heb#:**8518 תלה / ta-lah *(verb)*: Hang—To suspend with no support from below.

**Grk#:**4750 στομα / stom-a *(noun)*: Mouth *Freq:* 79
   **Heb#:**6310 פה / peh *(noun)*: Mouth—The opening through which food enters the body. Any opening.

**Grk#:**4757 στρατιωτης / strat-ee-o-tace *(noun)*: Soldier *Freq:* 26
   **Heb#:**1368 גיבור / gi-bor *(noun)*: Courageous—Having or characterized by mental or moral strength to venture, persevere, and withstand danger, fear or difficulty.

**Grk#:**4863 συναγω / soon-ag-o *(verb)*: Gather *Freq:* 62
   **Heb#:**6908 קבץ / qa-vats *(verb)*: Gather together—To come or bring into a group, mass or unit.

**Grk#:**4864 συναγωγη / soon-ag-o-gay *(noun)*: Synagogue *Freq:* 57
   **Heb#:**5712 עדה / ey-dah *(noun)*: Company—A group of persons or things for carrying on a project or undertaking;

---

[15] A 4th or 5th Century Aramaic New Testament.

a group with a common testimony. May also mean a witness or testimony.

**Heb#:**6951 קָהָל / qa-hal *(noun)*: Assembly—A large group, as a gathering of the flock of sheep to the shepherd.

**Grk#:**4893 συνειδησις / soon-i-day-sis *(noun)*: Conscience *Freq:* 32

**Heb#:**4093 מדע / ma-da *(noun)*: Insight—An intimacy with a person, idea or concept.

**Grk#:**4905 συνερχομαι / soon-er-khom-ahee *(verb)*: Come together *Freq:* 32

**Heb#:**622 אסף / a-saph *(verb)*: Gather—To bring together; to accumulate and place in readiness.

**Heb#:**6298 פגש / pa-gash *(verb)*: Encounter—To meet or come in contact with another person. A meeting between two hostile factions; to engage in conflict with.

**Heb#:**6908 קבץ / qa-vats *(verb)*: Gather together—To come or bring into a group, mass or unit.

**Grk#:**4920 συνιημι / soon-ee-ay-mee *(verb)*: Understand *Freq:* 26

**Heb#:**995 בין / bin *(verb)*: Understand—To grasp the meaning of; to have comprehension.

**Heb#:**7919 שכל / sa-khal *(verb)*: Calculate—To determine by mathematical deduction or practical judgment; to comprehend and carefully consider a path or course of action.

**Grk#:**4972 σφραγιζω / sfrag-id-zo *(verb)*: Seal *Freq:* 27
**Heb#:**2856 חתם / hha-tam *(verb)*: Seal—To close tightly, often marked with the emblem of the owner that must be broken before opening.

**Grk#:**4982 σωζω / sode-zo *(verb)*: Save *Freq:* 110
**Heb#:**3467 ישע / ya-sha *(verb)*: Rescue—To free or deliver from a trouble, burden or danger.

**Grk#:**4983 σωμα / so-mah *(noun)*: Body *Freq:* 146
**Heb#:**1472 גויה / ge-vi-yah *(noun)*: Body—By extension, the physical form, either alive or dead; a corpse.
**Heb#:**5315 נפש / ne-phesh *(noun)*: Being—The whole of a person, god or creature including the body, mind, emotion, character and inner parts.

**Grk#:**4990 σωτηρ / so-tare *(noun)*: Savior *Freq:* 24
**Heb#:**3467 ישע / ya-sha *(verb)*: Rescue—To free or deliver from a trouble, burden or danger. {The Greek word σωτηρ is a translation of the participle form of the Hebrew verb ישע meaning "one who rescues."}

**Grk#:**4991 σωτηρια / so-tay-ree-ah *(noun)*: Salvation *Freq:* 45
**Heb#:**3444 ישועה / ye-shu-ah *(noun)*: Relief—A deliverance or freedom from a trouble, burden or danger.

**Grk#:**5043 τεκνον / tek-non *(noun)*: Child *Freq:* 99
**Heb#:**1121 בן / ben *(noun)*: Son—A male offspring. This can be the son or a later male descendant of the father. One who continues the family line.

**Grk#:5048** τελειοω / tel-i-o-o *(verb)*: Make perfect *Freq:* 24
**Heb#:3634** כלל / ka-lal *(verb)*: Erect—To stand upright.
**Heb#:4390** מלא / ma-la *(verb)*: Fill—To occupy to the full capacity. {The Greek word τελειοω is a translation of the Hebrew word מלא when it is associated with the word יד *(yad,* Strong's Heb. #3027), meaning hand – fill the hand. This phrase is found in Exodus 28:41, where it is often translated as "consecrate."}

**Grk#:5055** τελεω / tel-eh-o *(verb)*: Finish *Freq:* 26
**Heb#:3615** כלה / ka-lah *(verb)*: Finish—To bring to an end; terminate; to complete an action, event.
**Heb#:8000** שלם / sha-lam *(verb)*: Make restitution—To restore or make right through action, payment or restoration to a rightful owner.

**Grk#:5056** τελος / tel-os *(noun)*: End *Freq:* 42
**Heb#:7097** קצה / qa-tsah *(noun)*: Extremity—The most distant end of something; the corner or edge.

**Grk#:5064** τεσσαρες / tes-sar-es *(adj)*: Four *Freq:* 42
**Heb#:702** ארבע / ar-ba *(noun)*: Four—A cardinal number.

**Grk#:5083** τηρεω / tay-reh-o *(verb)*: Keep *Freq:* 75
**Heb#:5341** נצר / na-tsar *(verb)*: Preserve—To watch over or guard for protection.
**Heb#:8104** שמר / sha-mar *(verb)*: Safeguard—The act or the duty of protecting or defending; to watch over or guard in the sense of preserving or protecting.

**Grk#:**5087 τιθημι / tith-ay-mee *(verb)*: Lay *Freq:* 96
**Heb#:**3322 יצג / ya-tsag *(verb)*: Leave—To put something in a place.
**Heb#:**5414 נתן / na-tan *(verb)*: Give—To make a present; to present a gift; to grant, allow or bestow by formal action.
**Heb#:**7760 שים / sim *(verb)*: Place—To put or set in a particular place, position, situation, or relation.

**Grk#:**5091 τιμαω / tim-ah-o *(verb)*: Honor *Freq:* 21
**Heb#:**3513 כבד / ka-vad *(verb)*: Be heavy—To be great in weight, wealth or importance. {The Greek word τιμαω is a translation of the piel (intensive) form of the Hebrew word כבד meaning "honor" in the sense of giving them weight.}

**Grk#:**5092 τιμη / tee-may *(noun)*: Honor *Freq:* 43
**Heb#:**3519 כבוד / ka-vod *(noun)*: Armament—The arms and equipment of a soldier or military unit. From a root meaning "heavy" and often paralleled with other weapons.
**Heb#:**6187 ערך / ey-rekh *(noun)*: Arrangement—Set in a row or in order according to rank or age. In parallel. Arranged items in juxtaposition.

**Grk#:**5095 Τιμοθεος / tee-moth-eh-os *(name)*: Timothy *Freq:* 28
**Heb#:**None טימותיוס / ti-mo-ti-os *(name)*: Tiymotiyos— A Hebrew transliteration of a personal name of Greek origin meaning "Honoring god."

**Grk#:**5103 Τιτος / tee-tos *(name)*: Titus *Freq:* 15
**Heb#:**None טיטוס / ti-tos *(name)*: Tiytos—A Hebrew transliteration of a personal name of Latin origin meaning "Nurse."

**Grk#:**5117 τοπος / top-os *(noun)*: Place *Freq:* 92
**Heb#:**4725 מקום / ma-qom *(noun)*: Area—An indefinite region or expanse; a particular part of a surface or body. A place.

**Grk#:**5140 τρεις / trice *(noun)*: Three *Freq:* 69
**Heb#:**7969 שלוש / she-losh *(noun)*: Three—A cardinal number.

**Grk#:**5154 τριτος / tree-tos *(adj)*: Third *Freq:* 57
**Heb#:**7992 שלישי / she-li-shi *(noun)*: Third—An ordinal number.

**Grk#:**5185 τυφλος / toof-los*(adj)*: Blind *Freq:* 53
**Heb#:**5787 עור / i-veyr *(noun)*: Blind—A darkness of the eye.

**Grk#:**5204 υδωρ / hoo-dore *(noun)*: Water *Freq:* 79
**Heb#:**4325 מים / ma-yim *(noun)*: Water—The Liquid of streams, ponds and seas or stored in cisterns or jars. The necessary liquid that is drunk.

**Grk#:**5207 υιος / hwee-os *(noun)*: Son *Freq:* 382
**Heb#:**1121 בן / ben *(noun)*: Son— A male offspring. This can be the son or a later male descendant of the father. One who continues the family line.

**Grk#:5217** υπαγω / hoop-ag-o *(verb)*: Go *Freq:* 81
    **Heb#:1980** הלך / ha-lakh *(verb)*: Walk—To move along on foot; walk a journey; to go. Also, customs as a lifestyle that is walked or lived.

**Grk#:5219** υπακουω / hoop-ak-oo-o *(verb)*: Obey *Freq:* 21
    **Heb#:8085** שמע / sha-ma *(verb)*: Hear—To perceive or apprehend by the ear; to listen to with attention. To obey.

**Grk#:5281** υπομονη / hoop-om-on-ay *(noun)*: Patience/Wait *Freq:* 32
    **Heb#:6960** קוה / qa-vah *(verb)*: Bound up—To be confined or hedged in together; to wait or to be held back in the sense of being bound up. {The Greek word υπομονη is a translation of the imperative form of the Hebrew verb קוה meaning "wait."}
    **Heb#:8615** תקוה / tiq-vah *(noun)*: Waiting—A standing still in anticipation or expectation.

**Grk#:5290** υποστρεφω / hoop-os-tref-o *(verb)*: Return *Freq:* 35
    **Heb#:7725** שוב / shuv *(verb)*: Turn back—To return to a previous place or state.

**Grk#:5293** υποτασσω / hoop-ot-as-so *(verb)*: Put under *Freq:* 40
    **Heb#:3533** כבש / ka-vash *(verb)*: Subdue—To conquer and bring into subjection; bring under control. Place the foot on the land in the sense of subduing it. Also, to place one's foot into another nation in the sense of subduing it.

**Grk#:5315** φαγω / fag-o *(verb)*: Eat *Freq:* 97
**Heb#:398** אכל / a-khal *(verb)*: Eat—To consume food; to destroy. A devouring of a fire.

**Grk#:5316** φαινω / fah-ee-no *(verb)*: Shine/Appear *Freq:* 31
**Heb#:215** אור / or *(verb)*: Light—To shine with an intense light; be or give off light; to be bright.

**Grk#:5319** φανεροω / fan-er-o-o *(verb)*: Make manifest *Freq:* 49
**Heb#:3045** ידע / ya-da *(verb)*: Know—To have an intimate and personal understanding; to have an intimate relationship with another person, usually sexual. {The Greek word φανεροω is a translation of the hiphil (causative) form of the Hebrew verb ידע meaning "to make known."}

**Grk#:5330** Φαρισαιος / far-is-ah-yos *(name)*: Pharisee *Freq:* 100
**Heb#:**None פרוש / pa-rush *(name)*: Parush—A proper name of Hebrew origin meaning "Scattered."

**Grk#:5342** φερω / fer-o *(verb)*: Bring *Freq:* 64
**Heb#:935** בוא / bo *(verb)*: Come—To move toward something; approach; enter. This can be understood as to come or to go. {The Greek word φερω is a translation of the hiphil (causative) form of the Hebrew verb בוא meaning "to make come," or "bring."}

**Grk#:5343** φευγω / fyoo-go *(verb)*: Flee *Freq:* 31
**Heb#:5127** נוס / nus *(verb)*: Flee—To run away, often from danger or evil; to hurry toward a place of safety; to flee to any safe place such as a city or mountain.

**Grk#:5346** φημι / fay-mee *(verb)*: Say *Freq:* 58
    **Heb#:559** אמר / a-mar *(verb)*: Say—To speak chains of words that form sentences.

**Grk#:5368** φιλεω / fil-eh-o *(verb)*: Love *Freq:* 25
    **Heb#:157** אהב / a-hav *(verb)*: Love—To provide and protect that which is given as a privilege. An intimacy of action and emotion. Strong affection for another arising from personal ties.

**Grk#:5376** Φιλιππος / fil-ip-pos *(name)*: Philip *Freq:* 38
    **Heb#:None** פילפוס / pil-pos *(name)*: Piylpos—A Hebrew transliteration of a personal name of Greek origin meaning "Lover of horses."

**Grk#:5384** φιλος / fee-los *(adj)*: Friend *Freq:* 29
    **Heb#:7453** רע / ra *(noun)*: Companion—One that accompanies another in the sense of a close companion or friend.

**Grk#:5399** φοβεω / fob-eh-o *(verb)*: Fear *Freq:* 93
    **Heb#:3372** ירא / ya-ra *(verb)*: Fear—To be afraid of; to have a strong emotion caused by anticipation or awareness of danger; the flowing or quivering of the gut from fear or awe; to dread what is terrible or revere what is respected.

**Grk#:5401** φοβος / fob-os *(noun)*: Fear *Freq:* 47
    **Heb#:367** אימה / ey-mah *(noun)*: Terror—A state of intense fear.
    **Heb#:3374** יראה / yi-rah *(noun)*: Fearfulness—Inclined to be afraid.

**Heb#:6343** פחד / pa-hhad *(noun)*: Awe—As trembling when in the presence of an awesome sight.

**Grk#:5426** φρονεω / fron-eh-o *(verb)*: Think *Freq:* 29
**Heb#:995** בין / bin *(verb)*: Understand—To grasp the meaning of; to have comprehension.

**Grk#:5438** φυλακη / foo-lak-ay *(noun)*: Prison *Freq:* 47
**Heb#:8104** שמר / sha-mar *(verb)*: Safeguard—The act or the duty of protecting or defending; to watch over or guard in the sense of preserving or protecting.

**Grk#:5442** φυλασσω / foo-las-so *(verb)*: Keep watch *Freq:* 30
**Heb#:5470** סוהר / so-har *(noun)*: Prison— A place of confinement.
**Heb#:8104** שמר / sha-mar *(verb)*: Safeguard—The act or the duty of protecting or defending; to watch over or guard in the sense of preserving or protecting. To keep watch.

**Grk#:5443** φυλη / foo-lay *(noun)*: Tribe *Freq:* 31
**Heb#:4294** מטה / ma-teh *(noun)*: Branch—A branch used as a staff. Also, a tribe as a branch of the family.
**Heb#:7626** שבט / she-vet *(noun)*: Staff—A walking stick made from the branch of a tree. Also, a tribe as a branch of the family.

**Grk#:5455** φωνεω / fo-neh-o *(verb)*: Call *Freq:* 42
**Heb#:7321** רוע / ru-a *(verb)*: Shout—To shout an alarm of war or for great rejoicing.

**Grk#:5456** φωνη / fo-nay *(noun)*: Voice *Freq:* 141
**Heb#:6963** קוֹל / qol *(noun)*: Voice—The faculty of utterance. Sound of a person, musical instrument, the wind, thunder, etc.

**Grk#:5457** φως / foce *(noun)*: Light *Freq:* 70
**Heb#:216** אוֹר / or *(noun)*: Light—The illumination from the sun, moon, stars, fire, candle or other source.

**Grk#:5463** χαιρω / khah-ee-ro *(verb)*: Rejoice *Freq:* 74
**Heb#:8056** שׂמח / sa-mahh *(adj)*: Rejoicing—A state of felicity or happiness.

**Grk#:5479** χαρα / khar-ah *(noun)*: Joy *Freq:* 59
**Heb#:4885** מסוֹס / ma-sus *(noun)*: Joy—A dancing around out of excitement.

**Grk#:5483** χαριζομαι / khar-id-zom-ahee *(verb)*: Forgive *Freq:* 23
**Heb#:2580** חן / hheyn *(noun)*: Beauty—The qualities in a person or thing that give pleasure to the senses. Someone or something that is desired, approved, favored or in agreement by another.

**Grk#:5485** χαρις / khar-ece *(noun)*: Grace *Freq:* 156
**Heb#:2580** חן / hheyn *(noun)*: Beauty—The qualities in a person or thing that give pleasure to the senses. Someone or something that is desired, approved, favored or in agreement by another.

**Grk#:5495** χειρ / khire *(noun)*: Hand *Freq:* 179
> **Heb#:3027** יד / yad *(noun)*: Hand—The terminal, functional part of the forelimb. Hand with the ability to work, throw and give thanks. Also euphemistically for the arm.

**Grk#:5503** χηρα / khay-rah *(noun)*: Widow *Freq:* 27
> **Heb#:490** אלמנה / al-ma-nah *(noun)*: Widow—A woman who has lost her husband by death. As bound in grief.

**Grk#:5505** χιλιας / khil-ee-as *(noun)*: Thousand *Freq:* 23
> **Heb#:505** אלף / e-leph *(noun)*: Thousand—Ten times one hundred in amount or number.

**Grk#:5506** χιλιαρχος / khil-ee-ar-khos *(noun)*: Captain *Freq:* 22
> **Heb#:441** אלוף / a-luph *(noun)*: Chief—Accorded highest rank or office; of greatest importance, significance, or influence. One who is yoked to another to lead and teach.
> **Heb#:8269** שר / sar *(noun)*: Noble—Possessing outstanding qualities or properties. Of high birth or exalted rank. One who has authority. May also mean "heavy" from the weight of responsibility on one in authority.

**Grk#:5532** χρεια / khri-ah *(noun)*: Need *Freq:* 49
> **Heb#:2656** חפץ / hhe-phets *(noun)*: Delight—An object or action that one desires.

**Grk#:5547** Χριστος / khris-tos *(adj)*: Christ *Freq:* 569
> **Heb#:4899** משיח / ma-shi-ahh *(noun)*: Smeared—Someone or something that has been smeared or

annointed with an oil as a medication or a sign of taking an office. An anointed one; a messiah.

**Grk#:5550** χρονος / khron-os *(noun)*: Time *Freq:* 53
    **Heb#:2165** זמן / z-man *(noun)*: Season—time set aside for a special occasion.
    **Heb#:3117** יום / yom *(noun)*: Day—The time between one dusk and the next one. Usually in the context of daylight hours but may also refer to the entire day or even a season.
    **Heb#:6256** עת / eyt *(noun)*: Appointed time—A fixed or officially set event, occasion or date.

**Grk#:5561** χωρα / kho-rah *(noun)*: Country *Freq:* 27
    **Heb#:776** ארץ / e-rets *(noun)*: Land—The solid part of the earth's surface. The whole of the earth or a region.
    **Heb#:7704** שדה / sa-deh *(noun)*: Field—An open land area free of trees and buildings. A level plot of ground, Pastureland.

**Grk#:5590** ψυχη / psoo-khay *(noun)*: Soul *Freq:* 105
    **Heb#:5315** נפש / ne-phesh *(noun)*: Being—The whole of a person, god or creature including the body, mind, emotion, character and inner parts.

**Grk#:5602** ωδε / ho-deh *(adv)*: Here *Freq:* 60
    **Heb#:2008** הנה / hey-nah *(adv)*: Thus far—The point beyond which something has not yet proceeded.

**Grk#:**5610 ωρα / ho-rah *(noun)*: Hour *Freq:* 108
    **Heb#:**8160 שעה / sha-a *(noun)*: Hour— A segment of time, the daylight divided into 12 equal segments, variable with the season and latitude.

# The Book of James (KJV with Strong's)

The Book of James has been included in this book to get you started with using this dictionary. Each English word is followed by its Strong's Greek number. Those Greek Strong's numbers that are not found within this dictionary are inside parentheses. Those Strong's Greek numbers that are not in parentheses are included in this dictionary and can be looked up to discover the Hebrew word and its definition behind the English words.

**1** James,G2385 a servantG1401 of GodG2316 and(G2532) of the LordG2962 JesusG2424 Christ,G5547 to the(G3588) twelve(G1427) tribesG5443 which(G3588) are scattered abroad,(G1722) (G1290) greeting.G5463 **2** My(G3450) brethren,G80 count(G2233) it all(G3956) joyG5479 when(G3752) ye fall into(G4045) divers(G4164) temptations;G3986 **3** KnowingG1097 *this,* that(G3754) the(G3588) trying(G1383) of your(G5216) faithG4102 workethG2716 patience.G5281 **4** But(G1161) let patienceG5281 have(G2192) *her* perfect(G5046) work,G2041 that(G2443) ye may be(G5600) perfect(G5046) and(G2532) entire,(G3648) wanting(G3007) nothing.(G3367) **5** (G1161) If(G1487) any(G5100) of you(G5216) lack(G3007) wisdom,G4678 let him askG154 of(G3844) God,G2316 that givethG1325 to all(G3956) *men* liberally,(G574) and(G2532) upbraideth(G3679) not;(G3361) and(G2532) it shall be givenG1325 him.(G846) **6** But(G1161) let him askG154 in(G1722) faith,G4102 nothing(G3367) wavering.(G1252) For(G1063) he that wavereth(G1252) is like(G1503) a wave(G2830) of the seaG2281 driven with the wind(G416) and(G2532) tossed.(G4494)

**7** For<sup>(G1063)</sup> let not<sup>(G3361)</sup> that<sup>(G1565)</sup> man<sup>G444</sup> think<sup>(G3633)</sup> that<sup>(G3754)</sup> he shall receive<sup>G2983</sup> any thing<sup>(G5100)</sup> of<sup>(G3844)</sup> the<sup>(G3588)</sup> Lord.<sup>G2962</sup> **8** A double minded<sup>(G1374)</sup> man<sup>G435</sup> *is* unstable<sup>(G182)</sup> in<sup>(G1722)</sup> all<sup>(G3956)</sup> his<sup>(G848)</sup> ways.<sup>G3598</sup> **9** <sup>(G1161)</sup> Let the<sup>(G3588)</sup> brother<sup>G80</sup> of low degree<sup>(G5011)</sup> rejoice<sup>G2744</sup> in<sup>(G1722)</sup> that he<sup>(G848)</sup> is exalted:<sup>(G5311)</sup> **10** But<sup>(G1161)</sup> the<sup>(G3588)</sup> rich,<sup>G4145</sup> in<sup>(G1722)</sup> that he<sup>(G848)</sup> is made low:<sup>(G5014)</sup> because<sup>(G3754)</sup> as<sup>(G5613)</sup> the flower<sup>(G438)</sup> of the grass<sup>(G5528)</sup> he shall pass away.<sup>G3928</sup> **11** For<sup>(G1063)</sup> the<sup>(G3588)</sup> sun<sup>G2246</sup> is no sooner risen<sup>(G393)</sup> with<sup>(G4862)</sup> a burning heat,<sup>(G2742)</sup> but<sup>(G2532)</sup> it withereth<sup>(G3583)</sup> the<sup>(G3588)</sup> grass,<sup>(G5528)</sup> and<sup>(G2532)</sup> the<sup>(G3588)</sup> flower<sup>(G438)</sup> thereof<sup>(G846)</sup> falleth,<sup>(G1601)</sup> and<sup>(G2532)</sup> the<sup>(G3588)</sup> grace<sup>(G2143)</sup> of the<sup>(G3588)</sup> fashion<sup>G4383</sup> of it<sup>(G846)</sup> perisheth:<sup>G622</sup> so<sup>(G3779)</sup> also<sup>(G2532)</sup> shall the<sup>(G3588)</sup> rich man<sup>G4145</sup> fade away<sup>(G3133)</sup> in<sup>(G1722)</sup> his<sup>(G848)</sup> ways.<sup>(G4197)</sup> **12** Blessed<sup>G3107</sup> *is* the man<sup>G435</sup> that<sup>(G3739)</sup> endureth<sup>(G5278)</sup> temptation:<sup>G3986</sup> for<sup>(G3754)</sup> when he is<sup>(G1096)</sup> tried,<sup>(G1384)</sup> he shall receive<sup>G2983</sup> the<sup>(G3588)</sup> crown<sup>(G4735)</sup> of life,<sup>G2222</sup> which<sup>(G3739)</sup> the<sup>(G3588)</sup> Lord<sup>G2962</sup> hath promised<sup>(G1861)</sup> to them that love<sup>G25</sup> him.<sup>(G846)</sup> **13** Let no man<sup>(G3367)</sup> say<sup>G3004</sup> when he is tempted,<sup>G3985</sup> I am tempted<sup>G3985</sup> of<sup>(G575)</sup> God:<sup>G2316</sup> for<sup>(G1063)</sup> God<sup>G2316</sup> cannot be tempted<sup>(G2076)</sup> <sup>(G551)</sup> with evil,<sup>G2556</sup> neither<sup>(G1161)</sup> tempteth<sup>G3985</sup> he<sup>(G848)</sup> any man:<sup>(G3762)</sup> **14** But<sup>(G1161)</sup> every man<sup>(G1538)</sup> is tempted,<sup>G3985</sup> when he is drawn away<sup>(G1828)</sup> of<sup>(G5259)</sup> his own<sup>(G2398)</sup> lust,<sup>G1939</sup> and<sup>(G2532)</sup> enticed.<sup>(G1185)</sup> **15** Then<sup>(G1534)</sup> when lust<sup>G1939</sup> hath conceived,<sup>(G4815)</sup> it bringeth forth<sup>(G5088)</sup> sin:<sup>G266</sup> and<sup>(G1161)</sup> sin,<sup>G266</sup> when it is finished,<sup>(G658)</sup> bringeth forth<sup>(G616)</sup> death.<sup>G2288</sup> **16** Do not<sup>(G3361)</sup> err,<sup>G4105</sup> my<sup>(G3450)</sup> beloved<sup>G27</sup> brethren.<sup>G80</sup> **17** Every<sup>(G3956)</sup> good<sup>G18</sup> gift<sup>(G1394)</sup> and<sup>(G2532)</sup> every<sup>(G3956)</sup> perfect<sup>(G5046)</sup> gift<sup>(G1434)</sup> is<sup>(G2076)</sup> from above,<sup>(G509)</sup> and cometh down<sup>G2597</sup> from<sup>(G575)</sup> the<sup>(G3588)</sup> Father<sup>G3962</sup> of lights,<sup>G5457</sup> with<sup>(G3844)</sup> whom<sup>(G3739)</sup> is<sup>(G1762)</sup> no<sup>(G3756)</sup> variableness,<sup>(G3883)</sup> neither<sup>(G2228)</sup> shadow<sup>(G644)</sup> of turning.(G5157) **18** Of his own will(G1014) begat(G616) he us(G2248) with the word(G3056) of truth,(G225) that we(G2248) should be(G1511) a kind(G5100) of firstfruits(G536) of his(G848) creatures.(G2938) **19** Wherefore,(G5620) my(G3450) beloved(G27) brethren,(G80) let every(G3956) man(G444) be(G2077) swift(G5036) to hear,(G191) slow(G1021) to speak,(G2980) slow(G1021) to(G1519) wrath:(G3709) **20** For(G1063) the wrath(G3709) of man(G435) worketh(G2716) not(G3756) the righteousness(G1343) of God.(G2316) **21** Wherefore(G1352) lay apart(G659) all(G3956) filthiness(G4507) and(G2532) superfluity(G4050) of naughtiness,(G2549) and receive(G1209) with(G1722) meekness(G4240) the(G3588) engrafted(G1721) word,(G3056) which is able(G1410) to save(G4982) your(G5216) souls.(G5590) **22** But(G1161) be(G1096) ye doers(G4163) of the word,(G3056) and(G2532) not(G3361) hearers(G202) only,(G3440) deceiving(G3884) your own selves.(G1438) **23** For(G3754) if any(G1536) be(G2076) a hearer(G202) of the word,(G3056) and(G2532) not(G3756) a doer,(G4163) he(G3778) is like unto(G1503) a man(G435) beholding(G2657) his(G846) natural(G1078) face(G4383) in(G1722) a glass:(G2072) **24** For(G1063) he beholdeth(G2657) himself,(G1438) and(G2532) goeth his way,(G565) and(G2532) straightway(G2112) forgetteth(G1950) what manner of man(G3697) he was.(G2258) **25** But(G1161) whoso looketh(G3879) into(G1519) the perfect(G5046) law(G3551) of(G3588) liberty,(G1657) and(G2532) continueth(G3887) *therein,* he(G3778) being(G1096) not(G3756) a forgetful(G1953) hearer,(G202) but(G235) a doer(G4163) of the work,(G2041) this man(G3778) shall be(G2071) blessed(G3107) in(G1722) his(G848) deed.(G4162) **26** If any man(G1536) among(G1722) you(G5213) seem(G1380) to be(G1511) religious,(G2357) and bridleth(G5468) not(G3361) his(G848) tongue,(G1100) but(G235) deceiveth(G538) his own(G848) heart,(G2588) this man's(G5127) religion(G2356) *is* vain.(G3152) **27** Pure(G2513) religion(G2356) and(G2532) undefiled(G283) before(G3844) God(G2316) and(G2532) the Father(G3962) is(G2076) this,(G3778) To visit(G1980) the fatherless(G3737) and(G2532)

New Testament Greek to Hebrew Dictionary

widows<sup>G5503</sup> in<sup>(G1722)</sup> their<sup>(G846)</sup> affliction,<sup>G2347</sup> *and* to keep<sup>G5083</sup> himself<sup>(G1438)</sup> unspotted<sup>(G784)</sup> from<sup>(G575)</sup> the<sup>(G3588)</sup> world.<sup>G2889</sup>

## Chapter 2

**1** My<sup>(G3450)</sup> brethren,<sup>G80</sup> have<sup>(G2192)</sup> not<sup>(G3361)</sup> the<sup>(G3588)</sup> faith<sup>G4102</sup> of our<sup>(G2257)</sup> Lord<sup>G2962</sup> Jesus<sup>G2424</sup> Christ,<sup>G5547</sup> *the Lord* of glory,<sup>G1391</sup> with<sup>(G1722)</sup> respect of persons.<sup>(G4382)</sup> **2** For<sup>(G1063)</sup> if<sup>(G1437)</sup> there come<sup>G1525</sup> unto<sup>(G1519)</sup> your<sup>(G5216)</sup> assembly<sup>G4864</sup> a man<sup>G435</sup> with a gold ring,<sup>(G5554)</sup> in<sup>(G1722)</sup> goodly<sup>(G2986)</sup> apparel,<sup>(G2066)</sup> and<sup>(G1161)</sup> there come in<sup>G1525</sup> also<sup>(G2532)</sup> a poor man<sup>G4434</sup> in<sup>(G1722)</sup> vile<sup>(G4508)</sup> raiment;<sup>(G2066)</sup> **3** And<sup>(G2532)</sup> ye have respect<sup>(G1914)</sup> to<sup>(G1909)</sup> him that weareth<sup>(G5409)</sup> the<sup>(G3588)</sup> gay<sup>(G2986)</sup> clothing,<sup>(G2066)</sup> and<sup>(G2532)</sup> say<sup>G2036</sup> unto him,<sup>(G846)</sup> Sit<sup>G2521</sup> thou<sup>(G4771)</sup> here<sup>G5602</sup> in a good place;<sup>G2573</sup> and<sup>(G2532)</sup> say<sup>G2036</sup> to the<sup>(G3588)</sup> poor,<sup>G4434</sup> Stand<sup>G2476</sup> thou<sup>(G4771)</sup> there,<sup>(G1563)</sup> or<sup>(G2228)</sup> sit<sup>G2521</sup> here<sup>G5602</sup> under<sup>(G5259)</sup> my<sup>(G3450)</sup> footstool:<sup>(G5286)</sup> **4** Are ye not then partial<sup>(G1252)</sup> <sup>(G3756)</sup> <sup>(G2532)</sup> in<sup>(G1722)</sup> yourselves,<sup>(G1438)</sup> and<sup>(G2532)</sup> are become<sup>(G1096)</sup> judges<sup>(G2923)</sup> of evil<sup>G4190</sup> thoughts?<sup>(G1261)</sup> **5** Hearken,<sup>G191</sup> my<sup>(G3450)</sup> beloved<sup>G27</sup> brethren,<sup>G80</sup> Hath not<sup>(G3756)</sup> God<sup>G2316</sup> chosen<sup>G1586</sup> the<sup>(G3588)</sup> poor<sup>G4434</sup> of this<sup>(G5127)</sup> world<sup>G2889</sup> rich<sup>G4145</sup> in<sup>(G1722)</sup> faith,<sup>G4102</sup> and<sup>(G2532)</sup> heirs<sup>(G2818)</sup> of the<sup>(G3588)</sup> kingdom<sup>G932</sup> which<sup>(G3739)</sup> he hath promised<sup>(G1861)</sup> to them that love<sup>G25</sup> him?<sup>(G846)</sup> **6** But<sup>(G1161)</sup> ye<sup>(G5210)</sup> have despised<sup>(G818)</sup> the<sup>(G3588)</sup> poor.<sup>G4434</sup> Do not<sup>(G3756)</sup> rich men<sup>G4145</sup> oppress<sup>(G2616)</sup> you,<sup>(G5216)</sup> and<sup>(G2532)</sup> draw<sup>(G1670)</sup> you<sup>(G5209)</sup> before<sup>(G1519)</sup> the judgment seats?<sup>(G2922)</sup> **7** Do not<sup>(G3756)</sup> they<sup>(G846)</sup> blaspheme<sup>G987</sup> that worthy<sup>G2570</sup> name<sup>G3686</sup> by the which<sup>(G3588)</sup> <sup>(G1909)</sup> ye<sup>(G5209)</sup> are called?<sup>G1941</sup> **8** If<sup>(G1487)</sup> ye<sup>(G3305)</sup> fulfil<sup>G5055</sup> the royal<sup>(G937)</sup> law<sup>G3551</sup> according<sup>(G2596)</sup> to the<sup>(G3588)</sup> scripture,<sup>G1124</sup> Thou shalt love<sup>G25</sup> thy<sup>(G4675)</sup> neighbour<sup>(G4139)</sup> as<sup>(G5613)</sup> thyself,<sup>(G4572)</sup> ye do<sup>G4160</sup> well:<sup>G2573</sup> **9** But<sup>(G1161)</sup> if<sup>(G1487)</sup> ye have respect to

112

persons,(G4380) ye commitG2038 sin,G266 and are convinced(G1651) of(G5259) the(G3588) lawG3551 as(G5613) transgressors.(G3848) **10** For(G1063) whosoever(G3748) shall keepG5083 the(G3588) wholeG3650 law,G3551 and(G1161) yet offend(G4417) in(G1722) oneG1520 *point*, he is(G1096) guilty(G1777) of all.(G3956) **11** For(G1063) he that said,G2036 Do not(G3361) commit adultery,(G3431) saidG2036 also,(G2532) Do not(G3361) kill.(G5407) Now(G1161) if(G1487) thou commit no adultery,(G3431) (G3756) yet(G1161) if thou kill,(G5407) thou art become(G1096) a transgressor(G3848) of the law.G3551 **12** So(G3779) speakG2980 ye, and(G2532) so(G3779) do,G4160 as(G5613) they that shall be(G3195) judgedG2919 by(G1223) the lawG3551 of liberty.(G1657) **13** For(G1063) he shall have judgmentG2920 without mercy,(G448) that hath shewedG4160 no(G3361) mercy;G1656 and(G2532) mercyG1656 rejoiceth against(G2620) judgment.G2920 **14** What(G5101) *doth it* profit,(G3786) my(G3450) brethren,G80 though(G1437) a man(G5100) sayG3004 he hath(G2192) faith,G4102 and(G1161) have(G2192) not(G3361) works?G2041 (G3361) canG1410 faithG4102 saveG4982 him?(G846) **15** (G1161) If(G1437) a brotherG80 or(G2228) sisterG79 be(G5225) naked,(G1131) and(G2532) destitute(G5600) (G3007) of daily(G2184) food,(G5160) **16** And(G1161) one(G5100) of(G1537) you(G5216) sayG2036 unto them,(G846) DepartG5217 in(G1722) peace,G1515 be *ye* warmed(G2328) and(G2532) filled;(G5526) notwithstanding(G1161) ye giveG1325 them(G846) not(G3361) those things which are needful(G2006) to the(G3588) body;G4983 what(G5101) *doth it* profit?(G3786) **17** Even(G2532) so(G3779) faith,G4102 if(G1437) it hath(G2192) not(G3361) works,G2041 is(G2076) dead,G3498 being alone.(G2596) (G1438) **18** Yea,(G235) a man(G5100) may say,G2046 Thou(G4771) hast(G2192) faith,G4102 and I(G2504) have(G2192) works:G2041 shewG1166 me(G3427) thy(G4675) faithG4102 without(G5565) thy(G4675) works,G2041 and I(G2504) will shewG1166 thee(G4671) my(G3450) faithG4102 by(G1537) my(G3450) works.G2041 **19** Thou(G4771) believestG4100 that(G3754) there is(G2076) one G1520 God; G2316 thou doest G4160 well: G2573 the(G3588) devils G1140 also(G2532) believe, G4100 and(G2532) tremble.(G5425) **20** But(G1161) wilt(G2309) thou know, G1097 O(G5599) vain(G2756) man, G444 that(G3754) faith G4102 without(G5565) works G2041 is(G2076) dead? G3498 **21** Was not(G3756) Abraham G11 our(G2257) father G3962 justified G1344 by(G1537) works, G2041 when he had offered(G399) Isaac G2464 his(G848) son G5207 upon(G1909) the(G3588) altar? G2379 **22** Seest G991 thou how(G3754) faith G4102 wrought with(G4903) his(G846) works, G2041 and(G2532) by(G1537) works G2041 was faith G4102 made perfect? G5048 **23** And(G2532) the(G3588) scripture G1124 was fulfilled G4137 which saith,(G3004 G1161) Abraham G11 believed G4100 God, G2316 and(G2532) it was imputed G3049 unto him(G846) for(G1519) righteousness: G1343 and(G2532) he was called G2564 the Friend G5384 of God. G2316 **24** Ye see G3708 then(G5106) how(G3754) that by(G1537) works G2041 a man G444 is justified, G1344 and(G2532) not(G3756) by(G1537) faith G4102 only.(G3440) **25** Likewise(G3668) also(G2532) was not(G3756) Rahab(G4460) the(G3588) harlot(G4204) justified G1344 by(G1537) works, G2041 when she had received(G5264) the(G3588) messengers, G32 and(G2532) had sent *them* out G1544 another G2087 way? G3598 **26** For(G1063) as(G5618) the(G3588) body G4983 without(G5565) the spirit G4151 is(G2076) dead, G3498 so(G3779) faith G4102 without(G5565) works G2041 is(G2076) dead G3498 also.(G2532)

## Chapter 3

**1** My(G3450) brethren, G80 be(G1096) not(G3361) many(G4183) masters, G1320 knowing(G1492) that(G3754) we shall receive G2983 the greater G3187 condemnation. G2917 **2** For(G1063) in many things(G4183) we offend(G4417) all.(G537) If any man(G1536) offend(G4417) not(G3756) in(G1722) word, G3056 the same(G3778) *is* a perfect(G5046) man, G435 *and* able G1415 also(G2532) to bridle(G5468) the(G3588) whole G3650 body. G4983

114

**3** Behold,(G2400) we put(G906) bits(G5469) in(G1519) the(G3588) horses'(G2462) mouths,(G4750) that they(G846) may obey(G3982) us;(G2254) and(G2532) we turn about(G3329) their(G846) whole(G3650) body.(G4983) **4** Behold(G2400) also(G2532) the(G3588) ships,(G4143) which though *they be*(G5607) so great,(G5082) and(G2532) *are* driven(G1643) of(G5259) fierce(G4642) winds,(G417) yet are they turned about(G3329) with(G5259) a very small(G1646) helm,(G4079) whithersoever(G3699) (G302) the(G3588) governor(G3730) (G2116) listeth.(G1014) **5** Even(G2532) so(G3779) the(G3588) tongue(G1100) is(G2076) a little(G3398) member,(G3196) and(G2532) boasteth great things.(G3166) Behold,(G2400) how great(G2245) a matter(G5208) a little(G3641) fire(G4442) kindleth!(G381) **6** And(G2532) the(G3588) tongue(G1100) *is* a fire,(G4442) a world(G2889) of iniquity:(G93) so(G3779) is(G2525) the(G3588) tongue(G1100) among(G1722) our(G2257) members,(G3196) that it defileth(G4695) the(G3588) whole(G3650) body,(G4983) and(G2532) setteth on fire(G5394) the(G3588) course(G5164) of nature;(G1078) and(G2532) it is set on fire(G5394) of(G5259) hell.(G1067) **7** For(G1063) every(G3956) kind(G5449) of beasts,(G2342) and(G2532) of birds,(G4071) and(G5037) of serpents,(G2062) and(G2532) of things in the sea,(G1724) is tamed,(G1150) and(G2532) hath been tamed(G1150) of mankind:(G442) (G5449) **8** But(G1161) the(G3588) tongue(G1100) can(G1410) no(G3762) man(G444) tame;(G1150) *it is* an unruly(G183) evil,(G2556) full(G3324) of deadly(G2287) poison.(G2447) **9** Therewith(G1722) (G846) bless(G2127) we God,(G2316) even(G2532) the Father;(G3962) and(G2532) therewith(G1722) (G846) curse(G2672) we men,(G444) which are made(G1096) after(G2596) the similitude(G3669) of God.(G2316) **10** Out(G1537) of the(G3588) same(G846) mouth(G4750) proceedeth(G1831) blessing(G2129) and(G2532) cursing.(G2671) My(G3450) brethren,(G80) these things(G5023) ought(G5534) not(G3756) so(G3779) to be.(G1096) **11** Doth(G3385) a fountain(G4077) send forth(G1032) at(G1537) the(G3588) same(G846) place(G3692) sweet(G1099) *water* and(G2532) bitter?(G4089) **12** (G3361) Can(G1410) the fig tree,(G4808) my(G3450) brethren,$^{G80}$ bear$^{G4160}$ olive berries?$^{(G1636)}$ either$^{(G2228)}$ a vine,$^{(G288)}$ figs?$^{(G4810)}$ so$^{(G3779)}$ *can* no$^{(G3762)}$ fountain$^{(G4077)}$ both yield$^{G4160}$ salt$^{(G252)}$ water$^{G5204}$ and$^{(G2532)}$ fresh.$^{(G1099)}$ **13** Who$^{(G5101)}$ *is* a wise man$^{G4680}$ and$^{(G2532)}$ endued with knowledge$^{(G1990)}$ among$^{(G1722)}$ you?$^{(G5213)}$ let him shew$^{G1166}$ out of$^{(G1537)}$ a good$^{G2570}$ conversation$^{(G391)}$ his$^{(G848)}$ works$^{G2041}$ with$^{(G1722)}$ meekness$^{(G4240)}$ of wisdom.$^{G4678}$ **14** But$^{(G1161)}$ if$^{(G1487)}$ ye have$^{(G2192)}$ bitter$^{(G4089)}$ envying$^{(G2205)}$ and$^{(G2532)}$ strife$^{(G2052)}$ in$^{(G1722)}$ your$^{(G5216)}$ hearts,$^{G2588}$ glory$^{(G2620)}$ not,$^{(G3361)}$ and$^{(G2532)}$ lie$^{(G5574)}$ not against$^{(G2596)}$ the$^{(G3588)}$ truth.$^{G225}$ **15** This$^{(G3778)}$ wisdom$^{G4678}$ descendeth$^{(G2718)}$ not$^{(G3756)}$ from above,$^{(G509)}$ but$^{(G235)}$ *is* earthly,$^{(G1919)}$ sensual,$^{(G5591)}$ devilish.$^{(G1141)}$ **16** For$^{(G1063)}$ where$^{(G3699)}$ envying$^{(G2205)}$ and$^{(G2532)}$ strife$^{(G2052)}$ *is,* there$^{(G1563)}$ *is* confusion$^{(G181)}$ and$^{(G2532)}$ every$^{(G3956)}$ evil$^{(G5337)}$ work.$^{(G4229)}$ **17** But$^{(G1161)}$ the$^{(G3588)}$ wisdom$^{G4678}$ that is from above$^{(G509)}$ is$^{(G2076)}$ first$^{G4412}$ $^{(G3303)}$ pure,$^{(G53)}$ then$^{(G1899)}$ peaceable,$^{(G1516)}$ gentle,$^{(G1933)}$ *and* easy to be intreated,$^{(G2138)}$ full$^{(G3324)}$ of mercy$^{G1656}$ and$^{(G2532)}$ good$^{G18}$ fruits,$^{G2590}$ without partiality,$^{(G87)}$ and$^{(G2532)}$ without hypocrisy.$^{(G505)}$ **18** And$^{(G1161)}$ the fruit$^{G2590}$ of righteousness$^{G1343}$ is sown$^{G4687}$ in$^{(G1722)}$ peace$^{G1515}$ of them$^{(G3588)}$ that make$^{G4160}$ peace.$^{G1515}$

# Chapter 4

**1** From whence$^{(G4159)}$ *come* wars$^{(G4171)}$ and$^{(G2532)}$ fightings$^{(G3163)}$ among$^{(G1722)}$ you?$^{(G5213)}$ *come they* not$^{(G3756)}$ hence,$^{(G1782)}$ *even* of$^{(G1537)}$ your$^{(G5216)}$ lusts$^{(G2237)}$ that war$^{(G4754)}$ in$^{(G1722)}$ your$^{(G5216)}$ members?$^{G3196}$ **2** Ye lust,$^{(G1937)}$ and$^{(G2532)}$ have$^{(G2192)}$ not:$^{(G3756)}$ ye kill,$^{(G5407)}$ and$^{(G2532)}$ desire to have,$^{(G2206)}$ and$^{(G2532)}$ cannot$^{G1410}$ $^{(G3756)}$ obtain:$^{(G2013)}$ ye fight$^{(G3164)}$ and$^{(G2532)}$ war,$^{(G4170)}$ yet$^{(G1161)}$ ye have$^{(G2192)}$ not,$^{(G3756)}$ because ye$^{(G5209)}$ ask$^{G154}$ not.$^{(G3361)}$ **3** Ye ask,$^{G154}$ and$^{(G2532)}$ receive$^{G2983}$ not,$^{(G3756)}$

because(G1360) ye ask(G154) amiss,(G2560) that(G2443) ye may consume(G1159) it upon(G1722) your(G5216) lusts.(G2237) **4** Ye adulterers(G3432) and(G2532) adulteresses,(G3428) know(G1492) ye not(G3756) that(G3754) the(G3588) friendship(G5373) of the(G3588) world(G2889) is(G2076) enmity(G2189) with God?(G2316) whosoever(G3739) (G302) therefore(G3767) will(G1014) be(G1511) a friend(G5384) of the(G3588) world(G2889) is(G2525) the enemy(G2190) of God.(G2316) **5** Do ye(G2228) think(G1380) that(G3754) the(G3588) scripture(G1124) saith(G3004) in vain,(G2761) The(G3588) spirit(G4151) that(G3739) dwelleth(G2730) in(G1722) us(G2254) lusteth(G1971) to(G4314) envy?(G5355) **6** But(G1161) he giveth(G1325) more(G3187) grace.(G5485) Wherefore(G1352) he saith,(G3004) God(G2316) resisteth(G498) the proud,(G5244) but(G1161) giveth(G1325) grace(G5485) unto the humble.(G5011) **7** Submit(G5293) yourselves therefore(G3767) to God.(G2316) Resist(G436) the(G3588) devil,(G1228) and(G2532) he will flee(G5343) from(G575) you.(G5216) **8** Draw nigh(G1448) to God,(G2316) and(G2532) he will draw nigh(G1448) to you.(G5213) Cleanse(G2511) your hands,(G5495) ye sinners;(G268) and(G2532) purify(G48) your hearts,(G2588) ye double minded.(G1374) **9** Be afflicted,(G5003) and(G2532) mourn,(G3996) and(G2532) weep:(G2799) let your(G5216) laughter(G1071) be turned(G3344) to(G1519) mourning,(G3997) and(G2532) your joy(G5479) to(G1519) heaviness.(G2726) **10** Humble yourselves(G5013) in the sight(G1799) of the(G3588) Lord,(G2962) and(G2532) he shall lift you up.(G5312) (G5209) **11** Speak not evil(G2635) (G3361) one of another,(G240) brethren.(G80) He that speaketh evil(G2635) of his brother,(G80) and(G2532) judgeth(G2919) his(G848) brother,(G80) speaketh evil(G2635) of the law,(G3551) and(G2532) judgeth(G2919) the law:(G3551) but(G1161) if(G1487) thou judge(G2919) the law,(G3551) thou art(G1488) not(G3756) a doer(G4163) of the law,(G3551) but(G235) a judge.(G2923) **12** There is(G2076) one(G1520) lawgiver,(G3550) who is able(G1410) to save(G4982) and(G2532) to destroy:(G622) who(G5101) art(G1488) thou(G4771) that(G3739) judgest(G2919) another?(G2087) **13** Go to(G33) now,(G3568) ye that say,G3004 To dayG4594 or(G2532) to morrow(G839) we will goG4198 into(G1519) such(G3592) a city,G4172 and(G2532) continueG4160 there(G1563) aG1520 year,(G1763) and(G2532) buy and sell,(G1710) and(G2532) get gain:(G2770) **14** Whereas(G3748) ye know(G1987) not(G3756) what(G3588) *shall be* on the(G3588) morrow.(G839) For(G1063) what(G4169) *is* your(G5216) life?G2222 It is(G2076) even(G1063) a vapour,(G822) that appeareth G5316 for(G4314) a little time,G3641 and(G1161) then(G1899) vanisheth away.(G853) **15** For(G473) that ye(G5209) *ought* to say,G3004 If(G1437) the(G3588) LordG2962 will,(G2309) we shall(G2532) live,G2198 and(G2532) doG4160 this,(G5124) or(G2228) that.(G1565) **16** But(G1161) now(G3568) ye rejoiceG2744 in(G1722) your(G5216) boastings:(G212) all(G3956) such(G5108) rejoicing(G2746) is(G2076) evil.G4190 **17** Therefore(G3767) to him that knoweth(G1492) to doG4160 good,G2570 and(G2532) doethG4160 *it* not,(G3361) to him(G846) it is(G2076) sin.G266

# Chapter 5

**1** Go to(G33) now,(G3568) *ye* rich men,G4145 weepG2799 and howl(G3649) for(G1909) your(G5216) miseries(G5004) that shall come upon(G1904) *you.* **2** Your(G5216) richesG4149 are corrupted,(G4595) and(G2532) your(G5216) garmentsG2440 are(G1096) motheaten.(G4598) **3** Your(G5216) gold(G5557) and(G2532) silver(G696) is cankered;(G2728) and(G2532) the(G3588) rust(G2447) of them(G846) shall be(G2071) a(G1519) witness(G3142) against you,(G5213) and(G2532) shall eatG5315 your(G5216) fleshG4561 as it were(G5613) fire.G4442 Ye have heaped treasure together(G2343) for(G1722) the lastG2078 days.G2250 **4** Behold,(G2400) the(G3588) hireG3408 of the(G3588) labourers(G2040) who have reaped down(G270) your(G5216) fields,G5561 which is of(G575) you(G5216) kept back by fraud,(G650) crieth:G2896 and(G2532) the(G3588) cries(G994) of them which have reapedG2325 are enteredG1525 into(G1519) the(G3588) ears(G3775) of the LordG2962 of sabaoth.(G4519) **5** Ye have lived in pleasure(G5171) on(G1909) the(G3588) earth,G1093 and(G2532) been wanton;(G4684) ye have nourished(G5142) your(G5216) hearts,G2588 as in(G1722) a dayG2250 of slaughter.(G4967) **6** Ye have condemned(G2613) *and* killed(G5407) the(G3588) just;G1342 *and* he doth not(G3756) resist(G498) you.(G5213) **7** Be patient(G3114) therefore,(G3767) brethren,G80 unto(G2193) the(G3588) comingG3952 of the(G3588) Lord.G2962 Behold,(G2400) the(G3588) husbandman(G1092) waiteth for(G1551) the(G3588) precious(G5093) fruitG2590 of the(G3588) earth,G1093 and(G2532) hath long patience(G3114) for(G1909) it,(G846) until(G2193) (G302) he receiveG2983 the early(G4406) and(G2532) latter(G3797) rain.(G5205) **8** Be ye also patient;(G3114) (G5210) (G2532) stablish(G4741) your(G5216) hearts:G2588 for(G3754) the(G3588) comingG3952 of the(G3588) LordG2962 draweth nigh.G1448 **9** Grudge(G4727) not(G3361) one against another,(G240) (G2596) brethren,G80 lest(G3363) ye be condemned:(G2632) behold,(G2400) the(G3588) judge(G2923) standethG2476 before(G4253) the(G3588) door.G2374 **10** Take,G2983 my(G3450) brethren,G80 the(G3588) prophets,G4396 who(G3739) have spokenG2980 in the(G3588) nameG3686 of the Lord,G2962 for an example(G5262) of suffering affliction,(G2552) and(G2532) of patience.(G3115) **11** Behold,(G2400) we count them happy(G3106) which endure.(G5278) Ye have heardG191 of the(G3588) patienceG5281 of Job,(G2492) and(G2532) have seen(G1492) the(G3588) endG5056 of the Lord;G2962 that(G3754) the(G3588) LordG2962 is(G2076) very pitiful,(G4184) and(G2532) of tender mercy.(G3629) **12** But(G1161) above(G4253) all things,(G3956) my(G3450) brethren,G80 swearG3660 not,(G3361) neither(G3383) by heaven,G3772 neither(G3383) by the(G3588) earth,G1093 neither(G3383) by anyG243 other(G5100) oath:(G3727) but(G1161) let your(G5216) yea(G3483) be(G2277) yea;(G3483) and(G2532) *your*(G3588) nay,(G3756) nay;(G3756) lest(G3363) ye fallG4098 into(G1519) condemnation.(G5272) **13** Is any among you

119

afflicted?(G2553) (G5100) (G1722) (G5213) let him pray.G4336 Is any merry?(G2114) (G5100) let him sing psalms.(G5567) **14** Is any sickG770 (G5100) among(G1722) you?(G5213) let him call forG4341 the(G3588) eldersG4245 of the(G3588) church;G1577 and(G2532) let them prayG4336 over(G1909) him,(G846) anointing(G218) him(G846) with oil(G1637) in(G1722) the(G3588) nameG3686 of the(G3588) Lord:G2962 **15** And(G2532) the(G3588) prayer(G2171) of faithG4102 shall saveG4982 the(G3588) sick,(G2577) and(G2532) the(G3588) LordG2962 shall raise him up;G1453 (G846) and if(G2579) he have(G5600) committedG4160 sins,G266 they shall be forgivenG863 him.(G846) **16** Confess(G1843) *your* faultsG3900 one to another,(G240) and(G2532) pray(G2172) one for another,(G240) (G5228) that(G3704) ye may be healed.G2390 The effectual ferventG1754 prayer(G1162) of a righteous manG1342 availeth(G2480) much.(G4183) **17** EliasG2243 was(G2258) a manG444 subject to like passions(G3663) as we(G2254) are, and(G2532) he prayed earnestlyG4336 G4335 that it might not(G3361) rain:(G1026) and(G2532) it rained(G1026) not(G3756) on(G1909) the(G3588) earthG1093 by the space of threeG5140 years(G1763) and(G2532) six(G1803) months.(G3376) **18** And(G2532) he prayedG4336 again,(G3825) and(G2532) the(G3588) heavenG3772 gaveG1325 rain,(G5205) and(G2532) the(G3588) earthG1093 brought forth(G985) her(G848) fruit.G2590 **19** Brethren,G80 if(G1437) any(G5100) of(G1722) you(G5213) do errG4105 from(G575) the(G3588) truth,G225 and(G2532) one(G5100) convertG1994 him;(G846) **20** et him know,G1097 that(G3754) he which convertethG1994 the sinnerG268 from(G1537) the error(G4106) of his(G846) wayG3598 shall saveG4982 a soulG5590 from(G1537) death,G2288 and(G2532) shall hide(G2572) a multitudeG4128 of sins.G266

# New Testament Greek to Hebrew Dictionary

# New Testament Greek to Hebrew Dictionary

# New Testament Greek to Hebrew Dictionary

# New Testament Greek to Hebrew Dictionary